WEEKEND WARDROBE

BY ANN LADBURY · DESIGNS BY CAROLINE CHARLES

BRITISH BROADCASTING CORPORATION

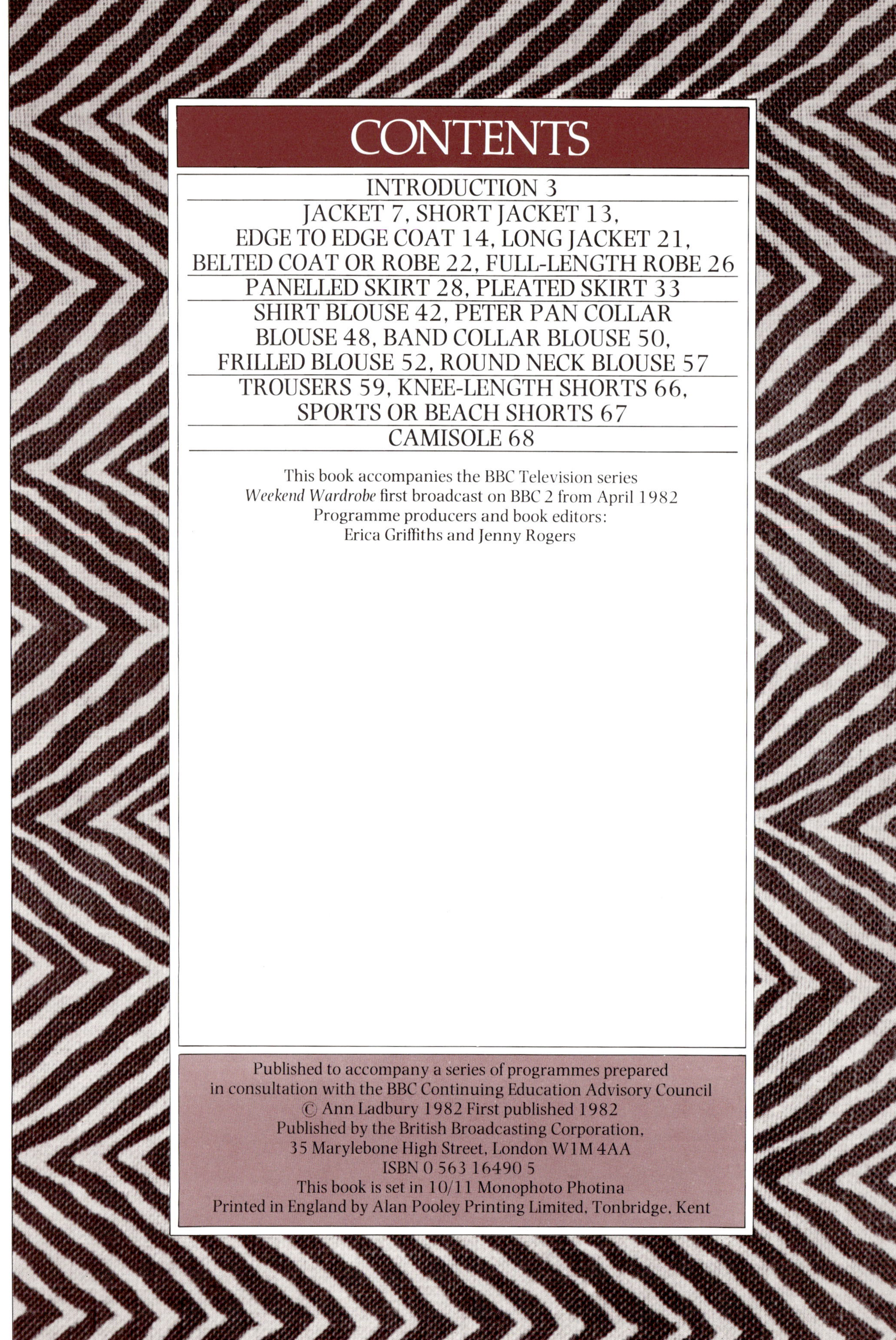

CONTENTS

This book accompanies the BBC Television series *Weekend Wardrobe* first broadcast on BBC 2 from April 1982
Programme producers and book editors:
Erica Griffiths and Jenny Rogers

Published to accompany a series of programmes prepared in consultation with the BBC Continuing Education Advisory Council

First published 1982
Published by the British Broadcasting Corporation, 35 Marylebone High Street, London W1M 4AA
ISBN 0 563 16490 5
This book is set in 10/11 Monophoto Photina
Printed in England by Alan Pooley Printing Limited, Tonbridge, Kent

INTRODUCTION

This book contains paper patterns and detailed instructions for making a versatile wardrobe of clothes. All the clothes have been designed for us by Caroline Charles, one of the most gifted of current London designers. She has chosen soft classic flattering shapes that are comfortable to wear and easy to make.

The basic wardrobe consists of six garments: jacket, two skirts, blouse, trousers and camisole. However, many variations are possible on these basic themes. We show 17 versions, but you will be able to work out many more for yourself.

Caroline Charles has designed the patterns so that they can be made up successfully in a wide variety of fabrics for summer or winter wear. For instance, the jacket can be made unlined in a sheer voile for evening but a lengthened version of the pattern will also produce a luxurious-looking lined tweed coat trimmed with fur. Similarly, the camisole can look glamorous in soft silk or sporty in towelling with matching beach shorts (using the short version of the trouser pattern). The trousers look as good in a sophisticated grey flannel for work as they do in a bright, lightweight cotton for leisure.

A blouse and skirt are basics in any wardrobe. There are two skirt patterns and both shapes will suit most figures. The blouse comes in five versions including a plain, classic shirt, a lightweight summer tunic and a ruffled, romantic style.

One of the advantages of doing your own sewing is that you can achieve the really excellent fit which is often elusive on ready-made clothes. This is why we have given detailed fitting hints in the instructions for each outfit. A good fit is essential if clothes are to be both flattering and comfortable so it is worth taking a little extra trouble at the early stages.

THE PATTERNS

The patterns in this book are multi-size from 10 to 18. The smaller sizes are all printed within the largest outline and each size is denoted by a different type of printed line. Locate your size and be sure to follow the same line right round each piece.

You will see that the sizes and lines only diverge at certain points: these are the vital areas of fit. In some places the size is the same for all the patterns: for example, seam pocket, width of cuff and waistband. Everywhere else the differences may look small but it is important that you use the correct dart size, tuck size, shoulder edge, sleeve head and so on, so that you start with the correct balance, even though you may want to make fitting adjustments later.

Seam and hem allowances are included and are marked at each edge. Remember to add more when cutting out if you want a deeper hem or a fuller skirt. If you do this, use tailor's chalk on the wrong side of the fabric to mark the amount added. This will remind you when you come to sew it.

What size pattern?

These are good basic patterns so use the one nearest to your own measurements. If you fall between two sizes choose the smaller size and, for safety, add a little extra side-seam allowance. All the patterns conform to the following body measurements:

SIZE 10	
Bust	81 cm (32 in)
Waist	62 cm (24 in)
Hips	87 cm (34 in)
SIZE 12	
Bust	87 cm (34 in)
Waist	66 cm (26 in)
Hips	92 cm (36 in)
SIZE 14	
Bust	92 cm (36 in)
Waist	69 cm (27 in)
Hips	97 cm (38 in)
SIZE 16	
Bust	97 cm (38 in)
Waist	74 cm (29 in)
Hips	102 cm (40 in)
SIZE 18	
Bust	102 cm (40 in)
Waist	79 cm (31 in)
Hips	107 cm (42 in)

To make jackets, blouses and camisole – choose the pattern closest to your correct bust size.

To make trousers, skirts, coats and robes – choose the pattern closest to your hip size.

Using a multi-size pattern

Cut out your own size, trimming off the surplus paper and lay the pattern on the fabric. When you have used the pattern for the first time, you can go back to it and adjust it according to any fitting alterations you have made in the fabric. You are sure to want to use the pattern more than once so after making these alterations press each piece on to lightweight iron-on interfacing, re-press and you will have a set of reinforced basic patterns that will never deteriorate with use.

If you feel it is a pity to cut up the patterns, you can use lightest weight sew-in interfacing laid over the patterns to trace your size with a felt pen. Use a ruler for the straight lines. Trace all the piece-names and markings. Cut out the pieces and store them in labelled polythene bags.

Lengthening or shortening patterns

The correct place to do this is indicated on the patterns.

Shorten by pinning a pleat in the pattern piece along this line.

Lengthen by cutting the pattern open along the line then pinning an extra piece of paper behind. Measure the alteration and make identical changes on any matching pieces. Redraw outer edges if they have become distorted.

FABRIC QUANTITY

The amount of fabric needed for each garment is given in specific fabric widths. If your selected fabric is not quoted you can ask the shop assistant to give you an equivalent amount (they often have a chart to refer to). Alternatively you can work it out yourself. The easiest way is to chalk a line along the table representing the selvedges of a folded piece of fabric. Now lay out the pattern pieces and measure along the table edge. If you do a lot of sewing it is probably worth buying a cutting board which will have markings on it to help make these calculations.

People who are taller or shorter than average may need a slightly different amount of fabric. Check the pattern pieces and estimate the difference, remembering to subtract seam and hem allowances. To double check, you can compare a main pattern piece with an existing garment whose length you like.

CUTTING OUT

Preparation

Press the whole length of fabric if it is creased. Look at the cutting-out layout diagram and see whether the fabric is to be laid out with selvedges together. If so, leave fabric folded along the centre. If it is not to be folded evenly, you must press out any central crease. Where a design has large pattern

repeats make sure that each line is precisely placed, inserting pins at intervals along the selvedge.
One cut end of the length of fabric should be arranged so that the thread (or row of loops in the case of knitted fabric) is level when the fabric is folded, and at right angles to the selvedges. If it was torn off by the shop assistant it will be exactly straight, but if it was cut it is unlikely to be quite straight. Where the end is not even, rule a chalk line on the straight grain on the right side. Do not cut off the surplus at this stage, in case it leaves you short of fabric.

Folding
It is nearly always easier to work with the fabric folded right side out. You can easily see and therefore avoid, flaws or dirty marks, and also make sure of the position and direction of any printed designs. When you come to mark the vital matching points and assemble the pieces, it is easier if the right side of the pairs of fabric pieces is outside.
Sometimes pile fabrics such as velvet may be difficult to pin, but folded with the pile inside you will have the additional problem of the layers catching together and creeping.
Place the fabric on the table, rolling up any part that will hang over the end. Try to avoid using the floor: it is exhausting and you will get fluff or carpet fibre sticking to the fabric.

Placing the pattern
Put all the pattern pieces in position, making sure the straight grain arrow on the pattern is parallel with the selvedge or exactly on the thread or line of the fabric. Insert a pin at each end of the arrow to anchor each pattern piece.
Insert more pins in the main, large, pieces of pattern, ready to cut out. Leave all small pieces anchored as they are and cut as you need them. This way you are less likely to mislay small pieces. Also you can more easily make fitting adjustments involving the smaller pattern pieces as you go along.

Pinning and cutting out
Use only a few pins, inserting them diagonally to prevent the fabric lifting. Keep them well inside the edge of the paper. If you have a problem area on your figure, for instance large thighs, leave extra on those edges ruling a cutting line with tailor's chalk. Use large shears and cut boldly with the pattern to the right and the surplus fabric peeling away to the left (or reverse if you are left-handed). Cut as much as possible without moving the fabric, then carefully slide the rest round until you finish the cutting. Leave the smallest pattern pieces anchored in position until you need them and roll up the fabric.
The fabric quantities and layouts in this book are for cutting out the fabric 'with nap' – that is with the fabric pieces lying one way only. Many fabrics are 'one-way' if not in design then in the way they catch the light (e.g. satin, velvet, jersey). If you are using a plain woven fabric or one with a small all-over design you may be able to work out a more economical layout by dovetailing the pieces in both directions.

MARKING

The marks and symbols on the pattern need to be transferred to the fabric to help you fit the pieces together. It is not always necessary to transfer every marking. We have indicated the important ones in the instructions for each garment.

Points to mark
The guide marks that *must* be transferred to the fabric include darts, tucks, sleeve head points, pocket positions, openings and centre back and centre front lines. These last two may be fabric folds: to mark, work a row of tacking stitches exactly in the fold of fabric. Also remember to mark the corresponding folds of facing pieces when they are cut out later in construction. Centre back folds of collars must be marked with tacking too.

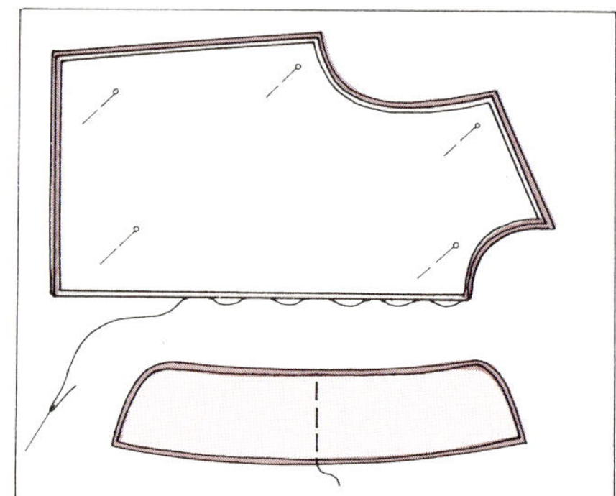

Transfer other marks by one of the following methods (on many patterns a combination of methods may be suitable):

Tracing wheel and carbon paper
This method marks two layers at once. Keep to orange or white paper in case the marks cannot be completely removed. Cut up the carbon paper into strips and fold them coloured-side out. Slip the strip between the two layers of fabric, wrong sides together, under the feature to be marked and run the tracing wheel over the pattern to be marked; pocket positions are more accurate if they have 'T' ends.
If the mark is required on the right side of the garment as well, run a row of tailor tackings or tacking along the carbon line.

Marking with chalk pencil
This marks one side only, one layer at a time: a good way of making a precise mark such as zip point or seam pocket point. You can mark right or wrong side of the fabric as the chalk brushes off easily.

Tailor's chalk
This is an alternative to the pencil. If two corresponding marks are needed you can rule a line on one piece of fabric, then place the other piece on top. Bang sharply with the flat of the hand and the mark will be found on both pieces. This is a useful way of making sure patch pockets are evenly placed.

Marking with tailor's tacks
This method marks two layers at once, both sides. It cannot harm the fabric but it takes a little longer. To mark darts or tucks, cut the pattern and fold back on the printed line. Use tacking thread and a larger hand sewing needle than for permanent sewing. Use the thread double but without a knot and take very small amounts of fabric on the needle beside the pattern edge. Take only one stitch, and leave a length of thread on the fabric about 2 cm ($\frac{3}{4}$ in) long before taking the next stitch. Do not leave raised loops of thread – they get caught up in your fingers and pull out too easily. Snip the loops of thread. Remove the pattern, part the layers of fabric and snip each stitch. These tiny double tufts of thread will remain in the fabric until you remove them.

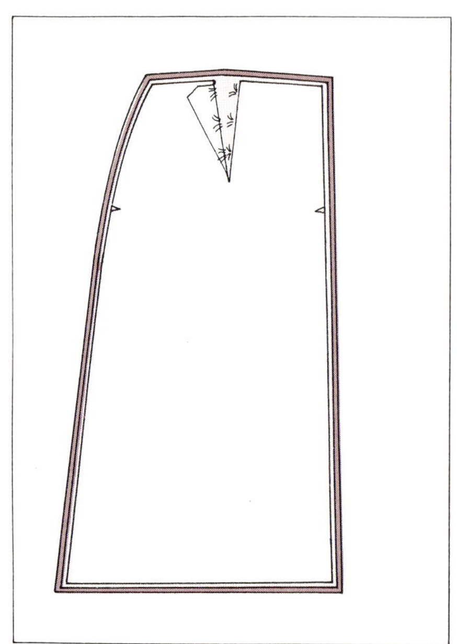

HANDSTITCHING

Handstitching can give neat, controlled finishing touches which you cannot achieve by machine. Each stitch has its own special function and the correct needle and thread is also important. Choose fine needles and fine thread for delicate fabrics, and so on. The best all-purpose needles for handsewing are 'betweens' which are sharp, short and come in a variety of sizes. Most handstitches are best started with a knot hidden in a fold or edge. Knots in thicker threads can be cut off later. When finishing off the stitching, use two neat backstitches worked on top of each other and concealed under a fold or edge.

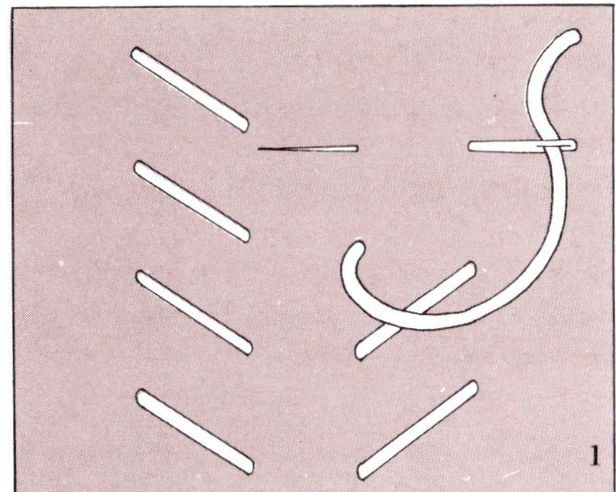

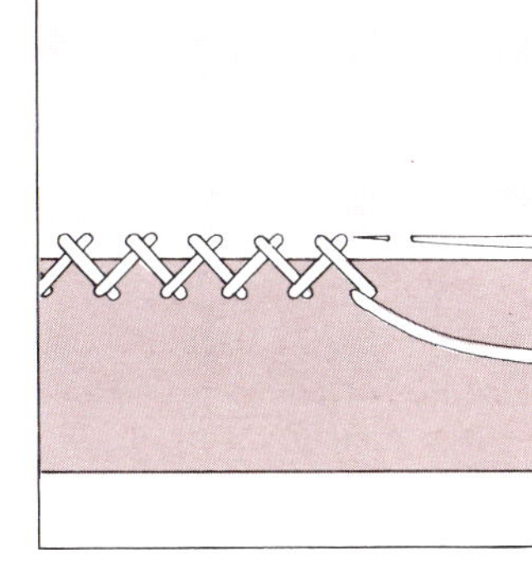

1 Basting
A large temporary diagonal stitch used to hold two pieces of fabric together. It can cover large areas quickly and holds fabric flat without the ridges which might otherwise occur. Working with the fabric flat on the table gives better results. Use tacking cotton, not ordinary sewing thread.

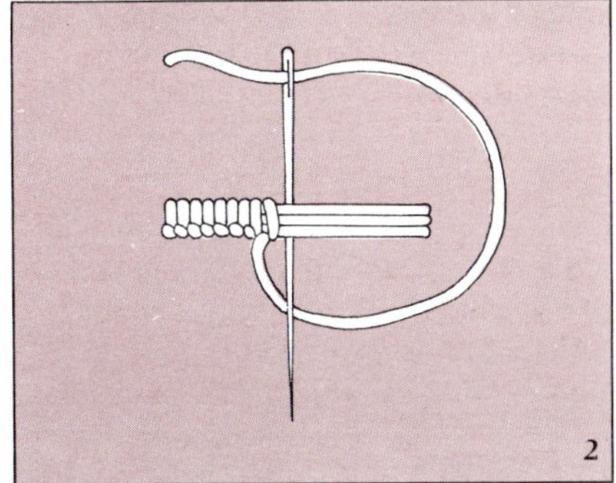

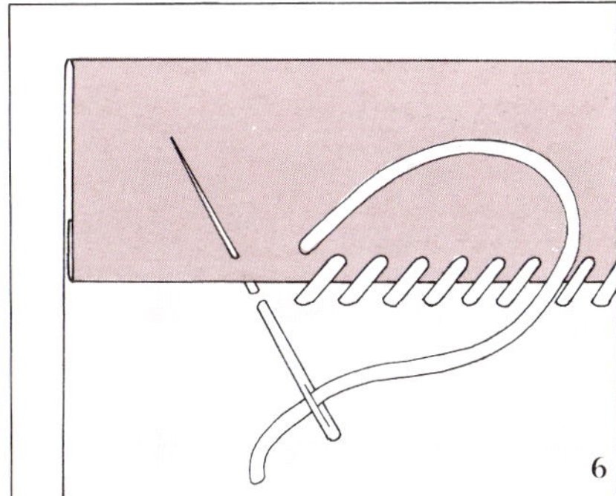

2 Bartack
This is a strengthening bar of stitches used to reinforce points of strain – e.g. pocket tops. A series of tiny loop stitches is worked over three horizontal threads. Whenever possible catch all the fabric layers.

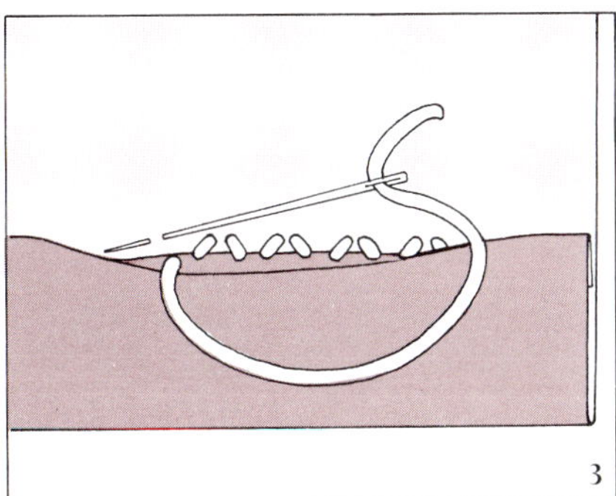

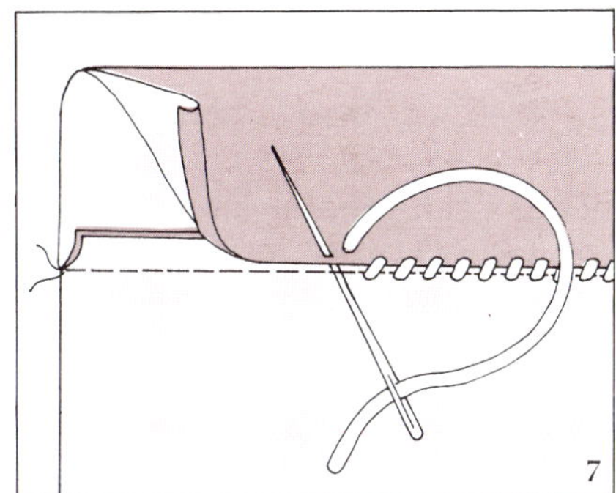

3 Catch stitch
Used for hems because it is invisible from the right side. Work it about 5 mm ($\frac{1}{4}$ in) under the hem edge to prevent a ridge. Try to pick up only one thread on the garment side and a little more on the hem itself. Keep the thread loose to avoid puckering.

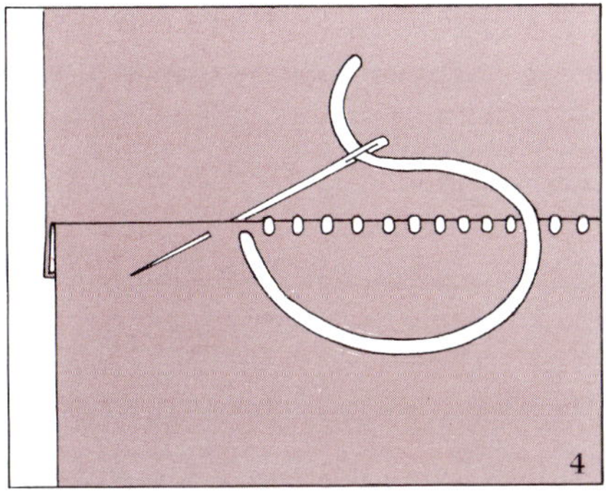

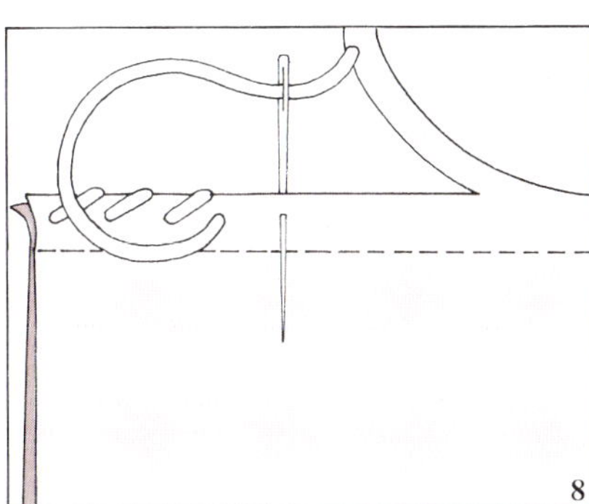

4 Felling
A strong tailoring stitch used for attaching linings to coats and jackets, or to hold down a fold of fabric.
To use with lining: fold under raw edge of lining and baste in position. Take a tiny deep stitch into the garment and bring needle up into the folded edge of the lining. Insert the needle again slightly behind where the needle came out: this will give an almost invisible stitch. Pull the thread quite taut so that the stitch disappears but not so taut that the lining wrinkles. The stitches should be 2 mm ($\frac{1}{16}$ in) apart.

5 Herringbone
Useful for catching interfacings, holding down raw edges and facings. The stitches should be loose or they cause a ridge. Work from left to right.

6 Hemming
Used for holding down a folded edge. It usually shows on the right side, so is not suitable for skirt and sleeve hems. The less of the single fabric you pick up, the less will show on the right side.

7 Hemming into machining
This is stronger and neater. Instead of picking up fabric, pick up the thread of machine stitching then start needle towards fabric fold pulled quite tightly.

8 Overcasting
A simple stitch used as an alternative to machine zig-zag for neatening raw edges. Don't pull the thread too tightly otherwise the edges will curl. Work quickly and make the stitches in shallow slants.

9 Prick stitch
A fairly strong type of backstitch used

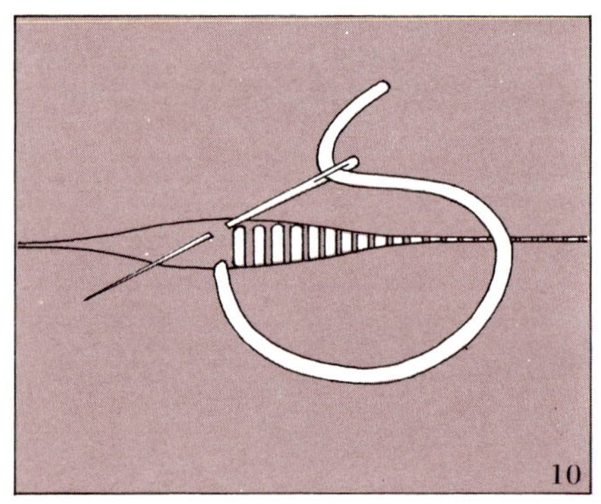

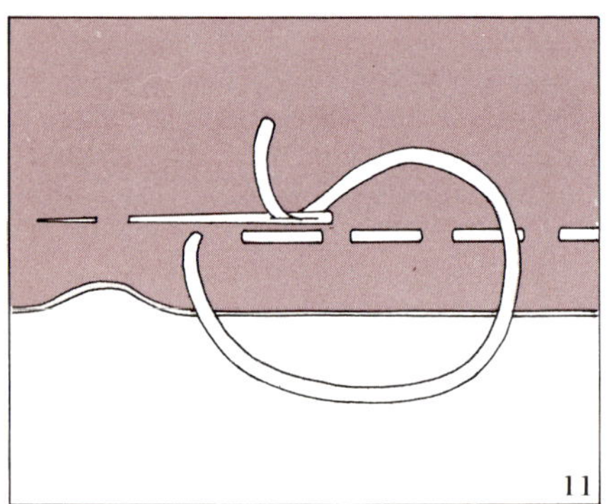

where machining would look ugly – e.g. to stitch through a seam join on the right side of faced bands. This stitch tends to look untidy on the wrong side, but is almost invisible from the right side. The stitches should be the shortest distance apart allowed by the fabric. Do not pull the thread too tightly.

10 Slip stitch
An invaluable stitch for joining two folded edges – e.g. the gap in a belt or the hem edges of faced bands on a jacket. Press the edges first. Pull the thread tightly enough to join the folds without wrinkling them, taking tiny stitches alternately in each fold.

11 Tacking
A temporary stitch used to mark lines or to hold two layers of fabric together for fitting and before machining. Always use tacking thread because its softness means it clings to the fabric firmly until you are ready to remove it. Always start with a knot and pick up as little fabric as possible on each stitch. Finish with a back stitch. Pull knot gently to remove.

INTERFACING

Interfacing prolongs the life and improves the general appearance of a garment. Insert it in edges, such as necklines and hems in order to prevent stretching or curling and also to improve hang and add weight. Its use also prevents excessive wear – for instance in buttonholes.
Interfacing can be woven or non-woven, sew-in or iron-on. The tendency now is to select iron-on varieties because they are quicker to use and are successful on all but a few delicate fabrics. The lightest weight interfacing is the most successful on all light and medium fabrics. If you have the lightest weight you can always build it up by using two layers, but a too heavy interfacing will ruin a garment. Many interfacings have to be cut on the same grain as the garment piece.

How to interface entire features (pockets, collars, bands, belts)
Pin pattern to folded interfacing. Cut out. Use a tracing wheel and carbon paper and transfer the essential markings listed in each section on making up the garments. If you are using iron-on interfacing, make a mark on the smooth non-adhesive side. Attach each piece of interfacing to the wrong side of the area of fabric that you have reserved for it.

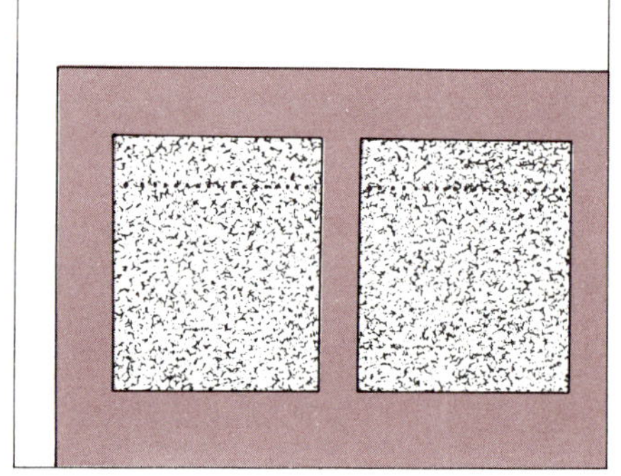

Sew-in interfacing should be basted down; iron-on should be pressed with a medium-hot iron and using a damp cloth if necessary. Cut out round each piece of interfacing.

How to interface selected areas (back neck, front edges, etc)
Pin facing pattern pieces to folded interfacing and cut round neck edge and garment edge. Using tracing wheel and folded carbon paper mark a line parallel with outer edge of facing but 2cm ($\frac{3}{4}$in) inside it to transfer a cutting line on to the interfacing. Transfer any other markings. Remove pattern. Cut out the pieces on the carbon lines. Cutting the interfacing smaller ensures that when it is in position it will be covered completely by the garment facing.
Frequent washing tends to detach iron-on interfacings at the free edge but they can be replaced by pressing back carefully when ironing.

Attaching interfacing
You must attach interfacing to the fabric of the *garment* to achieve the best results. Attaching interfacing to facings stiffens them, making them 'pop out' in wear because they are heavier than the garment. But do try out the interfacing on a spare piece of fabric first to make sure it does not show or affect the surface texture.

How to interface enclosed areas of strain (cuffs, waistbands)
Use either iron-on banding that has central perforations and edges to guide you (available in waistband weight and a lighter weight for cuffs); or use conventional interfacing of suitable weight. For waistbands only, use petersham, belt-backing or other waistband stiffening.

Quantities of interfacing
We have not quoted specific quantities in the instructions as these will vary according to the fabric you choose. Also, interfacing comes in too many differing widths to make sensible quotations. Measure the relevant pattern pieces and calculate your needs.

TOP STITCHING

Many garments in this book can be decorated with top stitching. It is not too difficult if done carefully. First, it should be worked through two layers of fabric or through two layers plus interfacing, but not through too many bulky layers. An even result can only be achieved if the fabric is even in thickness. A thick piece sewn to a single layer can easily cause wrinkling under the pressure. Where possible, therefore, work the top stitching as early as possible and consider it only as decoration. Do not try to save a process by making it perform a function as well, although sometimes it can help to keep an edge flat.

Preparing the edge to be stitched
Press it well, remove unnecessary tacking. Never mark the line to be stitched with tacking. Thread the machine with a newly-wound spool.
If you opt for bold top stitching thread on the top, you must use a large size needle – e.g. 110(18).
Always top stitch from the right side. Work a practice row and adjust the stitch length until it looks right. Note the machine stitch used and keep the sample as a reminder, since you are unlikely to be able to do all the top stitching at once.
Begin by lowering the needle into the fabric at precisely the right point (mark with chalk if necessary) then lower foot and machine. Try to use the edge of the machine foot as a width guide. Finish off leaving long thread ends. Pass all ends to the wrong side and sew in to fasten off. Press.

JACKET

A cardigan-style basic jacket, hip length, with shoulder tucks and patch pockets. The jacket is gently shaped on the side seams. The edges are faced and edged with top stitching. We made it in grey flannel and teamed it with the panelled skirt (page 28) and the shirt-style blouse (page 42).

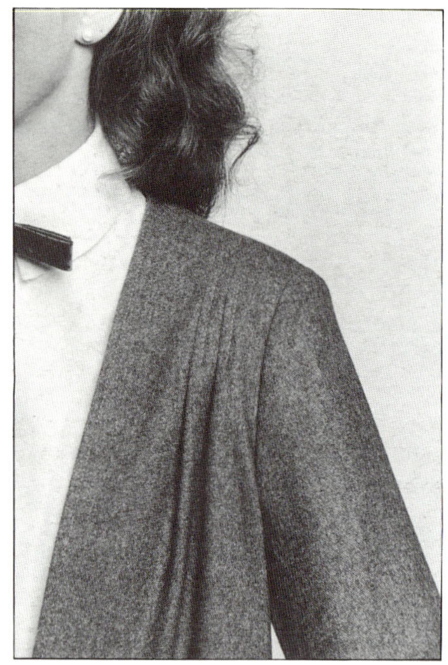

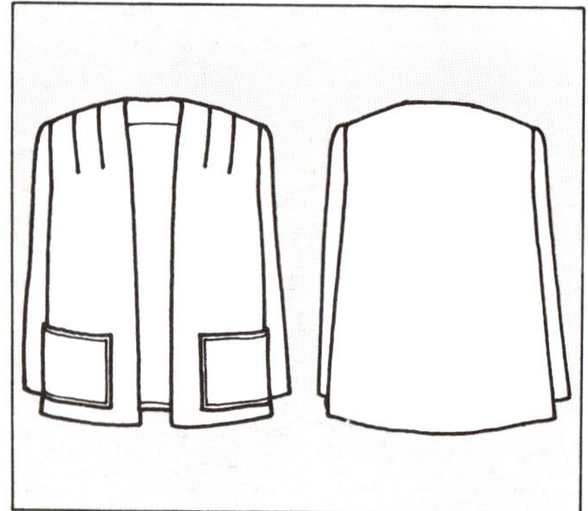

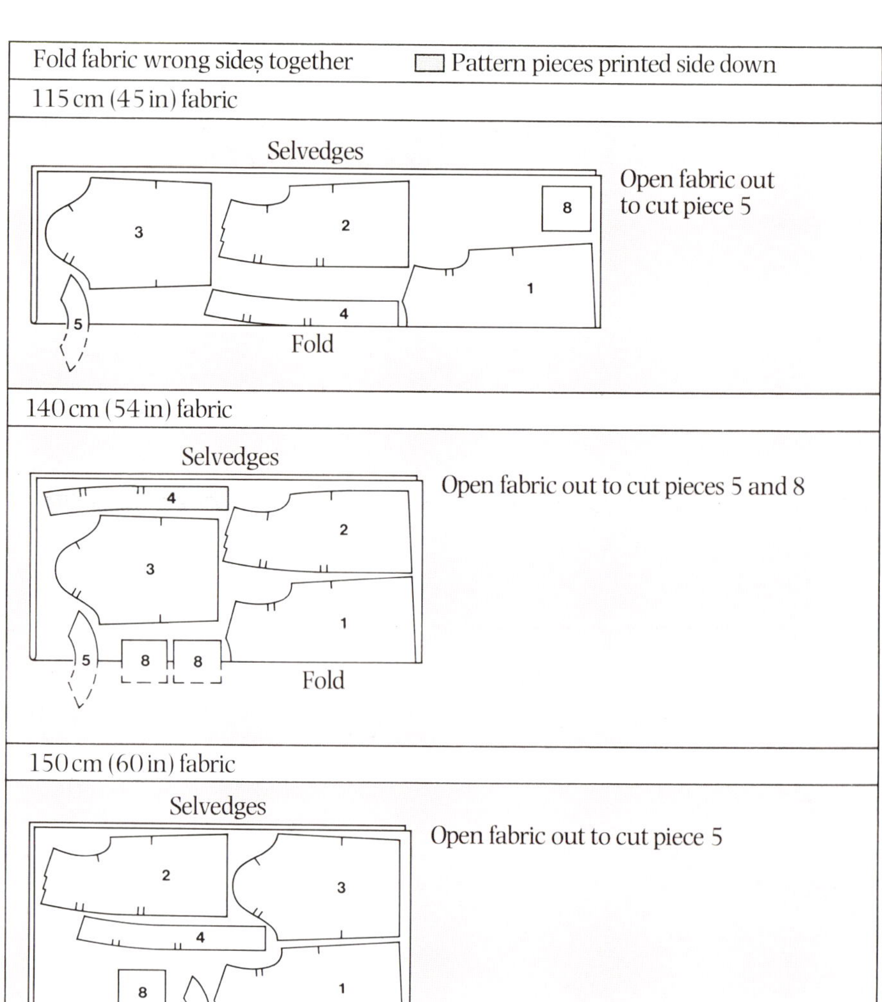

We have given very detailed fitting instructions for this jacket. If you make it up in an expensive fabric as an outer garment, it is worth taking trouble to achieve a really good fit.

You will need to refer to the following instructions when making any of the variations to the basic jacket pattern which follows on pages 13 to 27.
The colour photographs on the front and back cover show the jacket in grey flannel and in white sailcloth.

FABRIC

As well as grey flannel the jacket can be made in a variety of different fabrics such as blazer cloth, faced cloth, firm cotton, worsted, slub silk, bouclé or corduroy.

Quantities

Width	*Size*	*Quantity*
115cm (45in)	10	1.80m
	12	2.00m
	14	2.00m
	16	2.20m
	18	2.25m
140cm (54in)	10	1.45m
	12	1.50m
	14	1.50m
	16	1.50m
	18	1.55m
150cm (60in)	10	1.45m
	12	1.50m
	14	1.50m
	16	1.50m
	18	1.50m

If you want to line the jacket, buy the same quantity of lining as fabric and then follow the instructions for lining as described for the coat (page 15).
Interfacing is needed for back neck, front edges and pockets.
Finished length back neck to hem (size 12): 67cm ($26\frac{1}{2}$in).

HABERDASHERY

- 2 reels thread or 3 if top stitching is added
- Adhesive web to hold facings down
- 1 pair shoulder pads
- Small piece of lining
- Interfacing (see above)

PATTERN PIECES

1 and 2 traced to View B line on pattern plus 3, 4, 5 and 8.
Check and adjust if necessary length of 1, 2 and 3 and adjust facing length to correspond.

CUTTING OUT

Cut 4, 5 and 8 in interfacing.
Pin all pattern pieces on fabric and cut out 1, 2 and 3. Leave 4, 5 and 8 to be cut out when needed.
If using iron-on interfacing cut piece 8 (pocket), press it to the fabric and then cut round.

Marking
Mark centre back fold, balance marks on sleeve head and armholes; mark tucks and pocket positions.
Mark pocket top position on right side of jacket fronts using either chalk or chalk pencil.

MAKING UP

Attach interfacing to wrong side of jacket back and fronts.

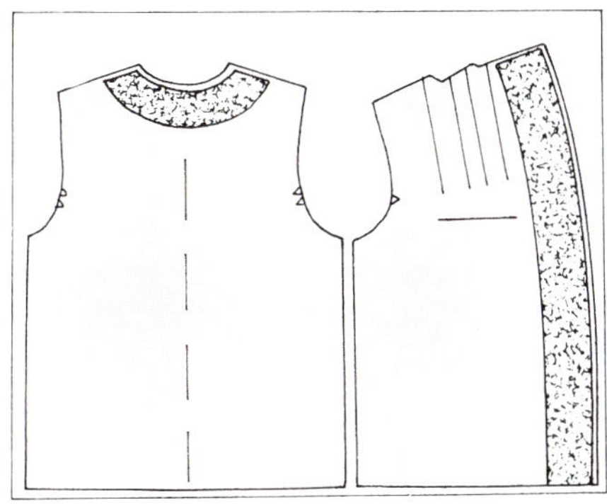

1 Shoulder tucks
Fold fabric right sides together and match up the tuck markings. Insert two pins across each tuck. Tack from base to shoulder edge. Remove pins. Machine on tacking from shoulder to base mark; fasten off the stitching. Remove tackings. Press stitching, then press the tucks so that the bulk lies towards the neckline. Press again, lightly, on the right side. Top stitch the tucks using the machine foot as a width guide (optional).

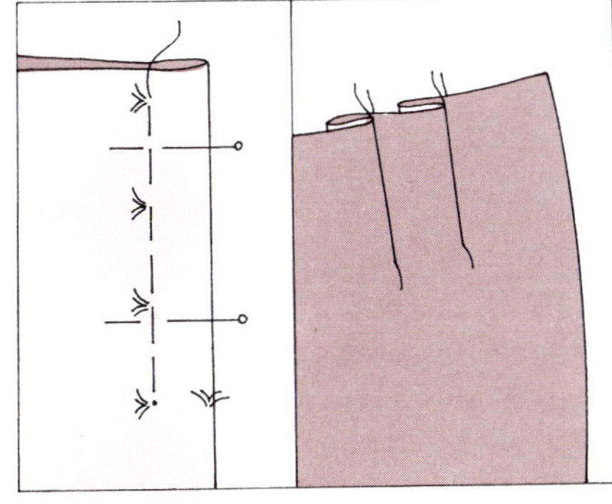

2 Shoulder seams
Tack shoulder and side seams.
Fit Try on jacket, slip shoulder pads into position and check the following: If the back neck is too wide make two very small darts 4 cm ($1\frac{1}{2}$ in) long. Remember there is still a seam allowance to be taken off the neck edge.
If the back of the jacket droops at the hemline or if diagonal folds appear near the armhole, lift the back only at the shoulders. Experiment by pinning along the entire shoulder seam and also by pinning only at shoulder edge, until the jacket hangs straight and clear of the body. If you do not wish to use shoulder pads (and remember they improve both fit and hang) you may have to lift the jacket and pin a new shoulder line to remove any folds of fullness in the armhole.
If you have sloping or square shoulders re-pin to fit the shoulder seams smoothly.
Look at the front of the jacket. Make sure the front edges are hanging vertically. If they swing out, lift the front at the shoulder at the neck edge only. Take note of any adjustments that may be needed at the side seams. They should hang vertically. If they need releasing snip the tacking and insert a pin to indicate the amount of release. If you are slim-hipped, reduce the jacket width by the amount necessary.
Remove jacket. Mark any side seam adjustment with tailor's chalk. Remove pins. At the shoulders, measure the amount of any pinned alteration, remove the pins, or re-insert them on the wrong side, then chalk a straight line on which to stitch. If the alteration was very extensive, re-tack the shoulders and try on the jacket again before stitching the seams.
Stitch and neaten the shoulder seams, using an open seam.

3 Open seam
Remove tacking and tailor tacks. Press the stitching flat then open the seam and arrange it wrong side up on a sleeve board. Run your finger firmly along it to flatten it then press. Use the iron lightly at first to open the seam and then more firmly. Turn the fabric over and press on the right side, using a muslin cloth to protect the fabric. Turn back to the wrong side and press once again.
Trim the raw edges a little and neaten with a small zig-zag stitch, or hand overcasting. The seam should not need repressing unless the machining tightens the edge. If it does, press the stitching only, holding the edge away from the garment.

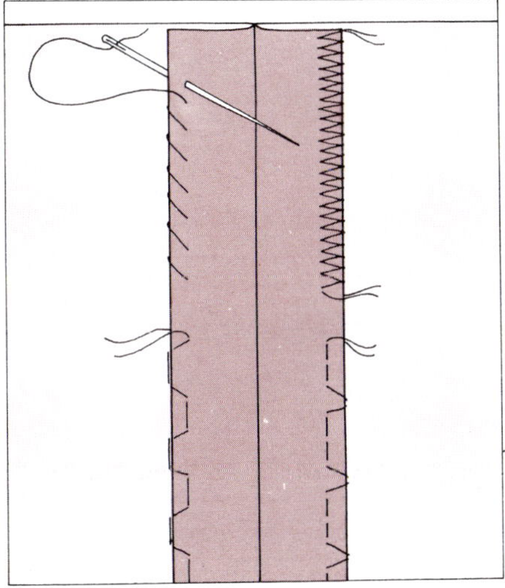

The double fold of fabric of the tucks may be bulky at the raw edge. Trim off the end of the tuck at an angle to make it easier to neaten the edge.

4 Facings
Place back neck facing right side down to right side jacket neck. Insert a couple of pins.
Place front facings to fronts of jacket and tack, starting from the hem and stopping about 3 cm ($1\frac{1}{4}$ in) from the shoulder seam.

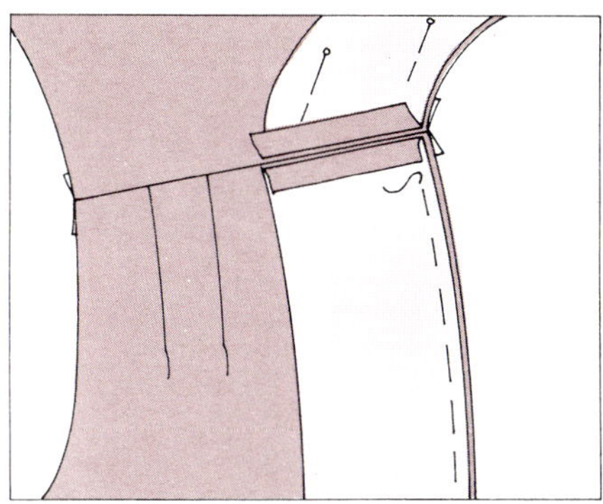

Working from jacket side, machine on this line of tacking to attach the front facings. Remove tackings.
Place jacket on a sleeve board right side up and with shoulder on the board. Arrange the ends of the back and front facings so that they meet when folded back.

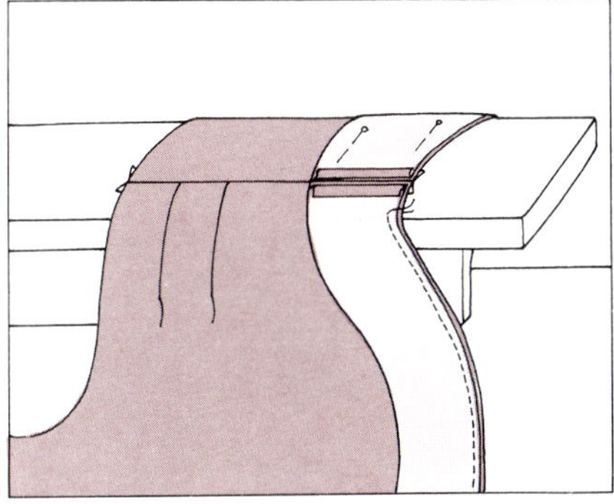

Press. Lift the edges and stitch with the press marks together, holding the facing away from the jacket. Press again then trim the surplus at the edges to 3 mm ($\frac{1}{8}$ in) or more if the fabric is thick.
Insert one pin across the facing join to hold it to the jacket. Turn jacket wrong side up and complete the stitching round the neck.

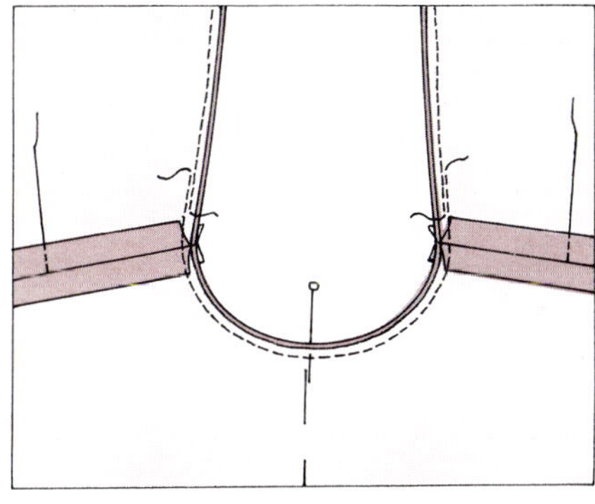

Remove all pins and tacking. Arrange jacket on sleeve board and press open the facing joins as far as possible.
Layer and trim the facing and jacket edges and roll the facings over to the inside. Work out the edges until the join is on the edge then, from the right side, roll and tack the jacket edge but push the join slightly out of sight.
Press the edge well from both sides.
Smooth out facing and baste in

position stopping basting well short of the hemline.

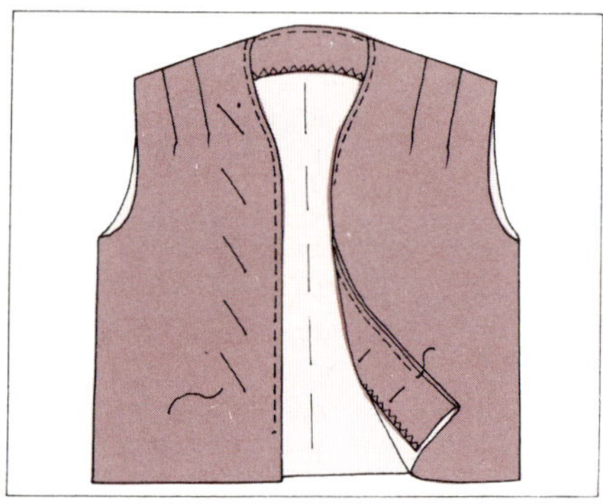

Trim and neaten the facing edge. Where it crosses the shoulder seams work herringbone stitch to hold it down. To hold the remainder of the facing in place slip short pieces of adhesive web between facing and jacket. Press. *Note* on lightweight fabric try this on a spare piece of fabric to make sure it does not show on the outside.

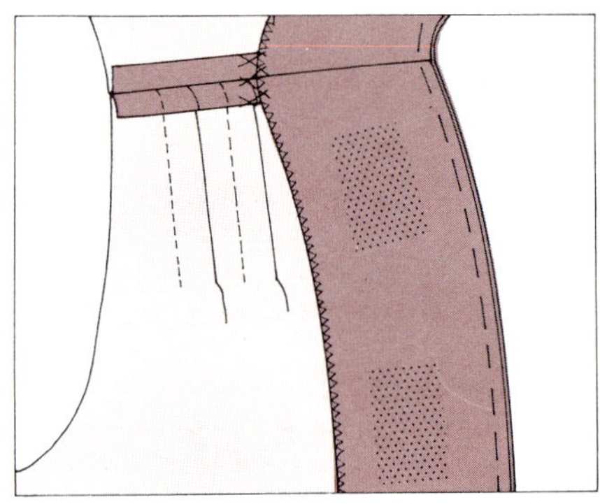

Leave the edge tacking in place until the garment is complete.

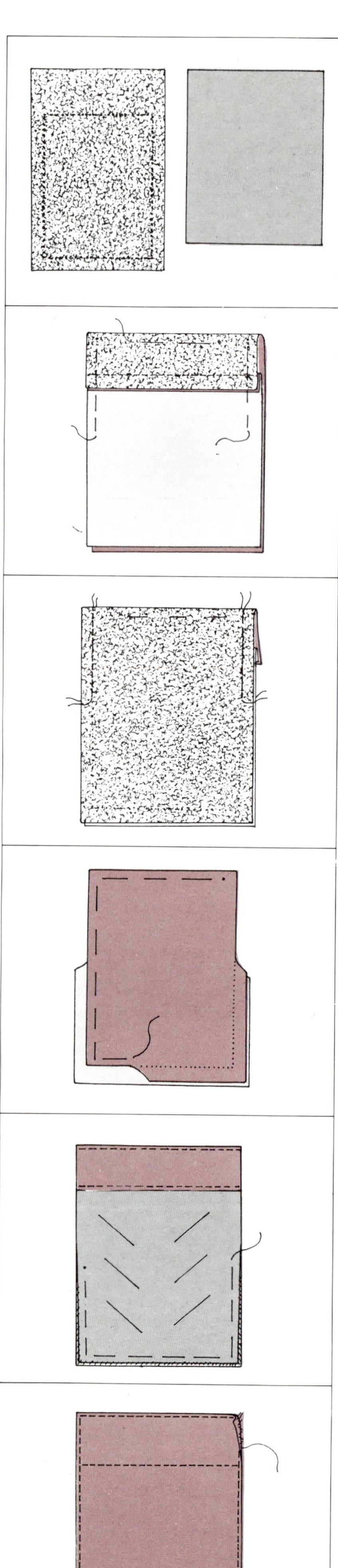

5 Patch pockets

Spread out the surplus fabric and cut out the pockets, cutting round the interfacing. The appearance and wear will be improved if they are lined. Use a piece of lining or cotton lawn. Cut a piece of lining for each pocket equal in width but 2.5cm (1 in) shorter in depth. Rule the exact pocket size on the interfacing and on right sides of each pocket, using tailor's chalk or chalk pencil.

Place lining to pocket with top edges together and right sides facing. Machine across the top. Press the join with both turnings towards the lining. Fold on pocket-top line, with lining and pocket right sides together. Insert a couple of tacking stitches to hold the fold. Tack down each side of the pocket to a little below the fabric edge. Turn pocket over so that interfacing is uppermost. Now follow your pocket markings. It is essential to make right-angled corners and parallel side edges. Machine both sides where tacked. Press the stitching. Trim and layer the lining and fabric turnings; cut away all surplus fabric at the corners. Turn pocket right side out. Work out the edges and corners until the join shows at the edge. Hold pocket right side towards you, tack along top edge then down each side for 3cm ($1\frac{1}{4}$in) rolling the join slightly to the under side. Continue tacking down sides and across bottom, turning in the pocket edge on the chalk line.

Insert tackings near the fold but not so close that turnings spring up. On reaching the corner, turn up the lower edge then fold in the side over it because the edge is less visible when placed at the bottom. Press the pocket edges taking care not to crease the lining which is still loose. Inside the pocket trim down the raw edges 5mm ($\frac{1}{4}$in). If fabric is very bulky or springy, hold down these edges with herringbone stitch.

Baste lining to pocket. Trim 1cm ($\frac{3}{8}$in) from the edges of the lining then turn in and tack to the pocket with the lining almost 3mm ($\frac{1}{8}$in) back from the pocket edge. Press lining edge lightly and fell round attaching it to the pocket. Remove tacking and press on wrong and right side. Top stitching is optional: work one or two rows round the pocket and top.

Place pockets in position. Slip jacket over your shoulders to check position and adjust if necessary. Tack across the top and baste all round. Stitch in place with slip stitch worked just under the edge. Make a small bartack at each top corner. Press.

6 Side seams

Tack side seams right sides together taking 1.5cm ($\frac{5}{8}$in) seam allowance. With jacket right side up, push both the seam allowances in one direction underneath and tack again to hold flat, about 5mm ($\frac{1}{4}$in) from the seam line. Tack the seam of one sleeve with one row of tacking and 1.5cm ($\frac{5}{8}$in) seam allowance.

Fit Slip jacket on, put shoulder pads in position and, if possible, wear the skirt to be teamed with it.

Check width at underarm and hip making sure any adjustments were correct. Make any further alterations necessary, until the front and back hang evenly with vertical seams.

Slip the tacked-up sleeve on to your arm and pin it to the jacket at the shoulder, adjusting it until you find approximately the correct shoulder point for setting in the sleeve.

Turn up the sleeve hem to approximately the length you require and insert one pin. Sleeve length is a matter of preference; the hem may come to the wrist bone or down to the hand. Next look at the jacket length. Turn it

up near the sleeve hem and insert a pin. The best effect is to have sleeve and jacket hems at the same level. Adjust to see if this can be achieved without the jacket hem passing across the widest part of the figure.
Take off jacket. Make chalk marks at shoulder, sleeve hem and jacket hem and remove all pins. Remove second row of tacking holding seam flat. Machine and neaten sides using open seams.
Fold the jacket front edges and sides together. Pin through the chalk mark at the side seam and chalk on the pin on both sides.
Make a chalk mark at centre back, taking a level amount of hemline.
Mark both edges at the centre front. Remove pins.
Open out the jacket and arrange right side up. Open out the facings.
Work a row of tacking to mark the hem line following the chalk marks. Turn up, tack near the fold. Press lightly and tack again half way between fold and raw edge.

7 Sleeves and shoulder pads
Tack and machine the sleeve seams, using open seams. Finish and neaten the raw edges. Press.
Turn up and tack the hems of both sleeves. Arrange jacket right side out and place each sleeve beside its armhole right side out. Make sure the right and left sleeves correspond to the armholes. Either check the matching pairs of balance marks or make sure the larger part of the sleeve head is to the back of the garment. Work on the underarm section of each sleeve first.
On the jacket make a corresponding chalk mark on the other shoulder to match the one made at fitting.

Setting in sleeve
Hold garment and sleeve and place the sleeve seam to garment side seam right sides together and pin.
The two raw edges are similar in shape and will fit together easily if you hold the underarm sections of the sleeve and garment together and tack. The amount that can be reached easily will be about 8 cm (3 in) on each side of the seam. Fasten off tacking.

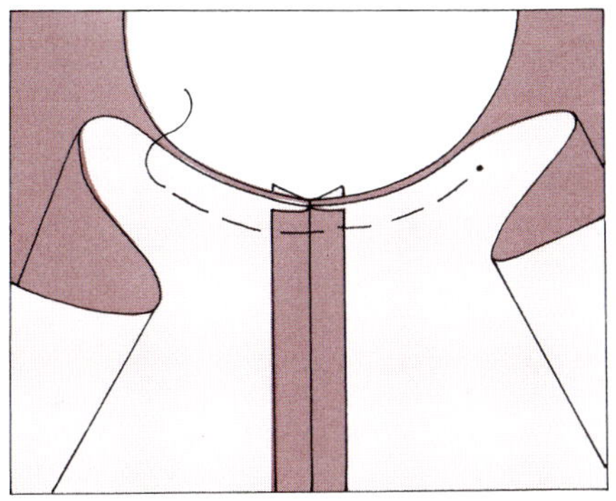

Tack right sleeve to right armhole and then tack left sleeve to left armhole. Put your hand inside the garment and take hold of the sleeve head and the top of the garment armhole at the shoulder seam. Holding the two together, pull them through and then turn them both over so that the sleeve is lying on top of the armhole but the edges are still together. Do not pull the whole of the sleeve through and do not turn the garment inside out.
Put the marked sleeve-head point to the shoulder seam and to chalk mark. Insert one pin across the sleeve head.

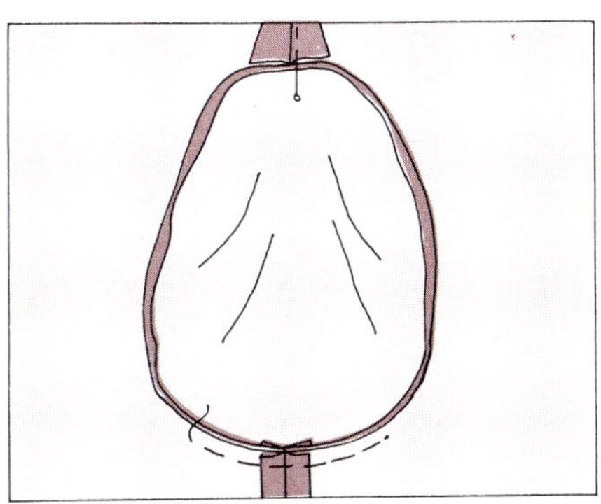

Move your hand to support one side of the sleeve head between this pin and the end of the tacking. Spread out your fingers under the two edges and pin. Start by inserting one pin in the centre of the area, then pin again in the middle. Continue putting in pins to divide up the ease. Any large amount of ease left undivided will form a pleat when stitched. Make sure the pins are close enough to prevent this.

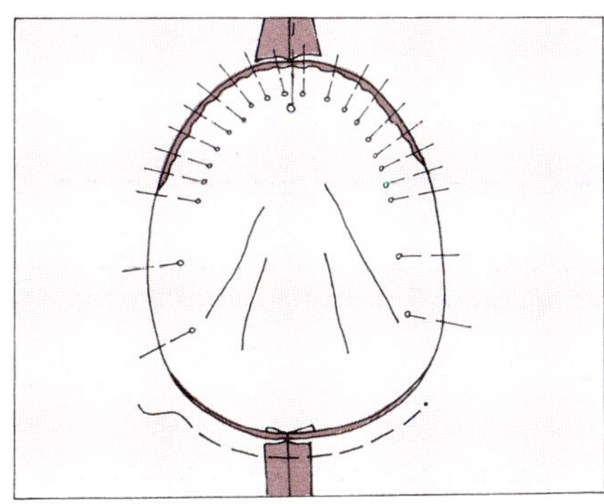

Move to the other side of the sleeve head and pin in the same way.
Turn garment so that sleeve is right side out and see how it hangs. Adjust pins if you can detect any obvious bulges of fullness.
Tack the sleeve head with small stitches. As you insert the needle under a pin, remove the pin and complete the stitch, insert the needle under the next pin and so on. Fasten off the tacking.
Put on the jacket and slip the shoulder pads into position.
The sleeve head seam should run straight down the armhole at front and back from the top of the shoulder bone. If it does not, snip the tacking on the sleeve head and adjust, bringing the sleeve head further up on the shoulder or further out along the shoulder seam. Do not try to pin the whole sleeve head but instead chalk a new line on the jacket shoulder area. Tack sleeve head in again to the new point and try on again.
The sleeve With your arm hanging in the natural position there should be no folds down or across the sleeve. If there are, snip the tacking to detach the sleeve and swivel it slightly in the armhole, moving the sleeve head point first to one side of the shoulder seam and then the other until it hangs straight. Correct both sleeves, holding the sleeve head to the jacket with one pin. Remove jacket, re-tack in new position and try on again.
With the sleeves tacked in position, bend your arm and move your shoulders slightly. If you feel any restriction at the back, snip the tacking in the back armhole and allow a small gap to open. Re-tack the sleeves and try on again.
Check the length of the sleeves, adjust if necessary. Also check the length of the jacket at this fitting. If you wish to alter it, remove tacking, re-tack at new level and try on again.

Inserting the sleeves
To stitch the sleeves into the armholes, use a medium size stitch, work with sleeve uppermost and machine very slowly beside the tacking stitches. If any part of the sleeve head begins to form a wrinkle, stop, use a pin to flatten it or snip the next tacking stitch and proceed. A 'free arm' machine makes this process easier.
Press from the right side with the turnings facing towards the sleeve to support the sleeve head. Insert a sleeve pad, ham or folded towel to support the sleeve and hold the whole jacket in one hand while pressing gently over the sleeve head. Do not press the underarm section.
Trim the raw edges to 1 cm ($\frac{3}{8}$ in) and neaten with zig-zag stitch or hand overcasting.

Sleeve hems
Press the tacked lower edge of sleeve. Prevent creasing by using a sleeve board or a folded towel in the sleeve. Turn sleeves wrong side out, trim raw edge evenly to no more than 4 cm ($1\frac{1}{2}$ in). Neaten by overcasting or zig-zag stitch. Finish by slipping a length of adhesive web under the edge making sure it is concealed. Now press carefully several times using a medium hot iron and damp cloth. Alternatively, tack the hem edge to

the sleeve just below the neatening. Lift the edge and finish by working catch stitch loosely between hem and sleeve. Remove tackings and press lightly from the right side. The iron must at no time rest heavily on the neatened edge or a mark will appear on the outside of the sleeve.
Top stitch hem the same distance from the edge as established for the shoulder tucks.

The shoulder pads
Use pads made from synthetic foam for washable jackets. Some foam shoulder pads are already covered with nylon jersey and can sometimes be used as they are. Uncovered pads should be covered by placing them on folded lining fabric. Put the thick edge of the pad against the fold of the fabric and chalk round the pad. Cut out the fabric, allowing a 5mm ($\frac{1}{4}$in) turning. Wrap the fabric round the pad and zig-zag round the outer edge. Alternatively, turn the raw edges to meet each other and hem together. This second method is best if the inside is likely to show.
To insert shoulder pads, hold jacket or coat over one hand right side out. Insert pad and position it so that the edge extends into the sleeve head by 5mm ($\frac{1}{4}$in). Insert a couple of pins through coat and pad. The pad should extend slightly further towards the back of the armhole than the front, in order to support the natural hollow that occurs there.
On the inside, work a bar tack 3mm ($\frac{1}{8}$in) long to attach the centre of the pad to the shoulder seam. At the armhole edge, lift the pad a little and work three spaced bar tacks between pad and armhole turnings.

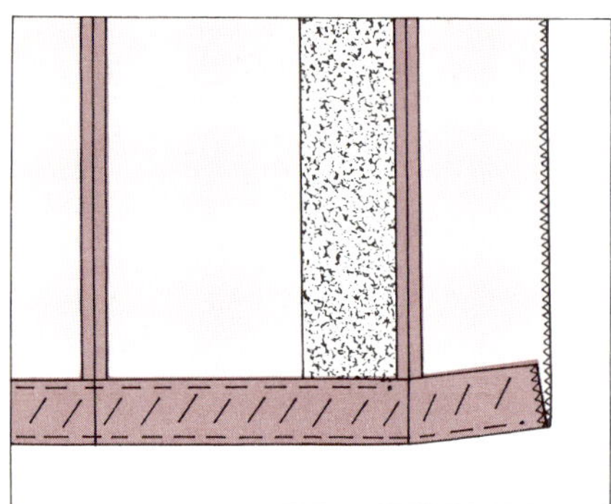

8 Jacket hem
Remove upper row of tacking in hem, leaving one row only near the fold. Press the fold where the facing extends. Make sure the join is open, then turn up the hem of the facing and tack, but angle the edge up slightly. Press the hem of the facing. Trim the hem edge neatly to a depth of 4cm ($1\frac{1}{2}$in).

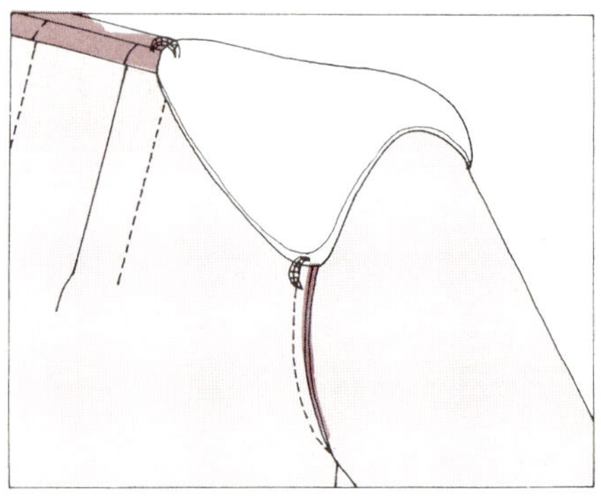

You could finish the hem by pressing in adhesive web with a damp cloth and medium-hot iron. Do not take web into the facing.
Alternatively, you could tack the neatened edge to the jacket and hold down by working catch stitch at the front edge.
To complete the jacket corners – both methods: at the facing join trim down the hem edge to 1cm ($\frac{3}{8}$in). Fold over the facing to the wrong side, tack the jacket edges and tack along the hem where the two folds will lie together but with the facing slightly back from the jacket edge. Make this corner very neat, adjusting the turned up edge of the facing if necessary. Remember the corners are seen from the outside so check the appearance. Press the corners from the right side, then finish by slip stitching the lower edge and working loopstitch or buttonhole stitch at the bottom where the facing crosses the hem.

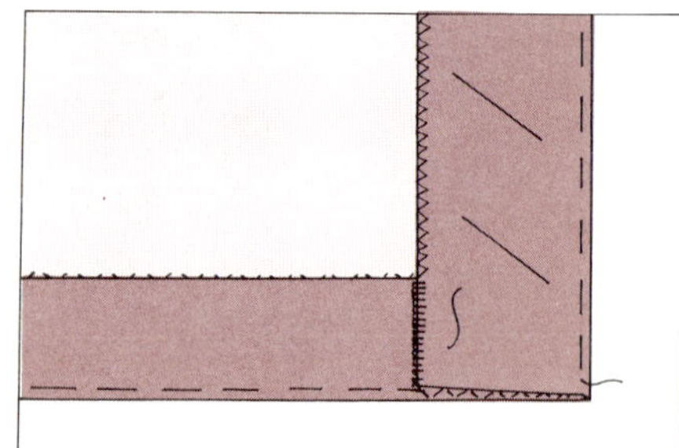

Top stitch front edges. Press jacket from right side.

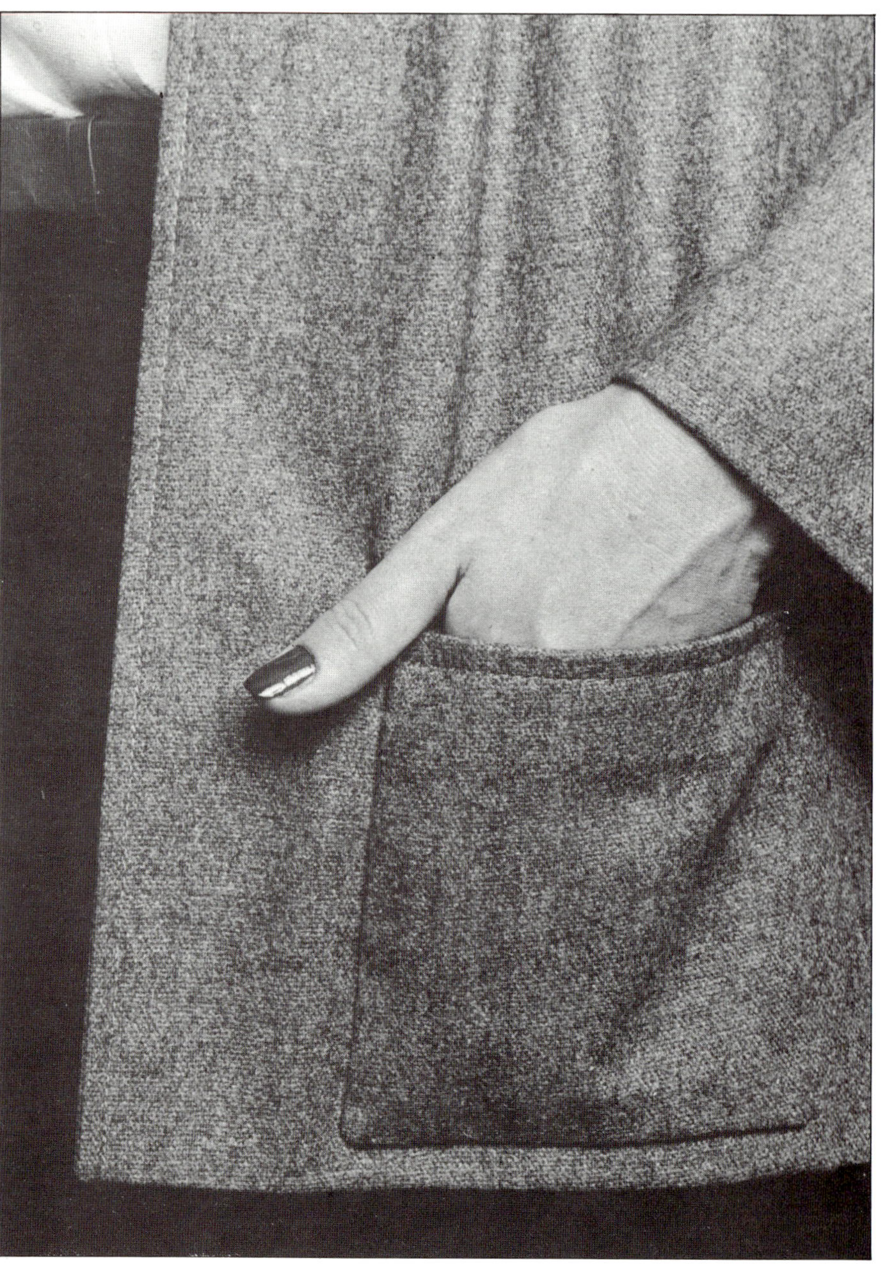

SHORT JACKET

The jacket here is cropped to just below the waist, to wear with skirt or trousers. We made it in black, grey and red checked fabric and teamed it with the pleated skirt (page 33) made in black wool crêpe and the shirt blouse (page 42) in white silk crêpe.

FABRIC

You could use any plain or patterned medium weight fabrics such as wool crêpe, jersey, suede, cotton drill, silk, viyella, wool challis or linen.

Quantities
Refer to the fabric quantities for the basic jacket on page 8 but as this jacket is 17cm ($6\frac{1}{2}$in) shorter, it takes a little less fabric.
If you use check fabric, allow for matching. Add an extra check for each of the main pattern pieces.
Interfacing is needed for back neck and front edges. Use light sew-in or iron-on interfacing.
Finished length back neck to waist (size 12): 50cm ($19\frac{1}{2}$in).

HABERDASHERY

As for the basic jacket, page 8.

PATTERN PIECES

1, 2 and 4 to short length (View A on pattern); 3 and 5.

CUTTING OUT

As for the basic jacket, but check fabric needs careful preparation if the pattern is to match exactly at the seams.
The end of the length of fabric must be trimmed exactly on a line of check.
Fold the fabric carefully, matching all lines down and across the fabric.
Insert pins all over the entire length at intervals of about 10cm (4in).
With a bold large check decide where the main line should fall on your figure, and draw a pencil line on the back jacket pattern. Put the front pattern beside it with side seam edges together and continue the line across the front. Place the sleeve pattern beside the front and extend the line on to it.
Place all pieces on the fabric, matching pencil lines to the check and

with all pieces lying in one direction on the straight grain.
Pin and cut out.

MAKING UP

Make up as basic jacket, page 8, but omit pockets. If using check fabric, use the following method of tacking seams to make sure the checks match. Fold under the seam allowance of one piece and lay it on the right side of the piece to match it. Insert a few pins and slip tack the seam. Take a small stitch in the fold followed by one in the flat piece, and so on. Remove pins. Open out the fabric and on the wrong side it will appear tacked as an open seam.

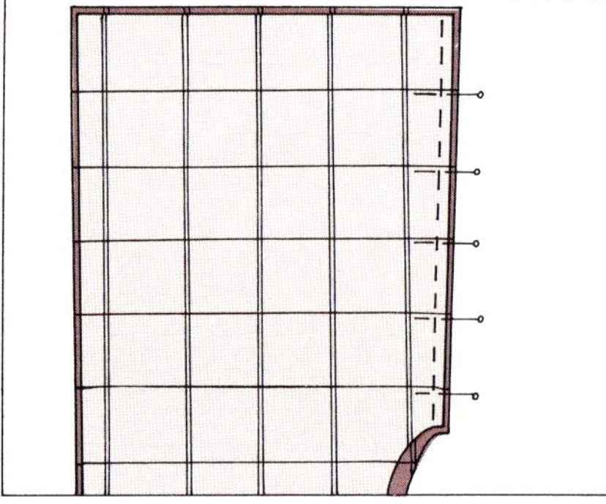

Insert pins across the seam, picking up the same part of the check on both layers. Machine, stitching slowly over the pins. This technique prevents the layers moving when stitching.

EDGE TO EDGE COAT

A luxurious coat made from the same pattern but fairly easy to make and elegant to wear. We made it in heavy herringbone tweed with astrakhan fur trimming, lined it and teamed it with the panelled skirt (page 28) in the same tweed to wear with the frilled blouse (page 52).

As this variation will probably be made up in an expensive fabric, it is worth taking trouble to achieve a really good fit. Refer closely to the detailed fitting instructions given for the basic jacket on page 9.

Fold fabric wrong sides together ☐ Pattern pieces printed side down

115 cm (45 in) fabric

Selvedges

3 7 2 6 10 9 9 1

Fold

140 cm (54 in) fabric

Selvedges

3 2 7 6 10 9 9 1

Fold

FABRIC

Use coat-weight fabric such as tweed, flannel, faced cloth, mohair, poodle cloth, quilted fabric, or use reversible cloth and omit lining. Use fur fabric or real fur for trimming or use a contrasting material.

Quantities

Width	*Size*	*Quantity*
115cm (45in)	10	3.25m
	12	3.30m
	14	3.30m
	16	3.30m
	18	3.30m
140cm (54in)	10	2.55m
	12	2.60m
	14	2.60m
	16	2.60m
	18	2.75m

You will need to work out how much fur is required. Some types must be used in one direction only and you may need a larger quantity because of this. Ours was a wide jersey-backed curly type 160cm (60in) wide with no one-way pile and so could be cut in either direction. But it was soft and required interfacing. Cutting bands and hem bands economically i.e. across the width, it took less than 30cm. If you use fur strip, calculate the total length required.
The bands on hem and sleeve are cut to 7cm (2¾in) wide.
Interfacing is needed for the bands, pockets, hemline and cuffs.
Use medium or heavy iron-on interfacing or a sew-in type if you cannot press the kind of fur you are using.
Buy the same quantity of lining as fabric.
Finished length back neck to hem: 113cm (44½in).

HABERDASHERY

3 reels thread

1 pair shoulder pads

A small piece of wadding for sleeve-head roll

Interfacing (see below left)

PATTERN PIECES

1, 2 and 3 adjusted to desired finished length plus 1.5cm (⅝in) seam allowance and 9 (band) adjusted to correspond; 6 and 7.
Make a copy of 7 (coat pocket tab) and cut it along the fold line

CUTTING OUT

Cut out 6 and 9 in interfacing and also the new half-width pocket tab, 7.
The bands on hem and sleeve are straight and can be cut directly in fur after measuring the garment. Mark fur on the wrong side with chalk and cut pieces singly rather than pinning on the pattern pieces.
Cut real fur and thick-pile synthetic fur with a trimming knife or razor blade, cutting through backing only.
Cut 1, 2, 3 and 9 in fabric to the line marked View D on the pattern and also the half-width pocket tab, 7. Open out fabric and press pocket interfacings, 6, to wrong side and cut out.

Marking
Mark centre back fold, tucks, armhole and sleeve head markings.
Mark balance marks on coat front edge.
Mark pocket position on right and wrong sides.

MAKING UP

1 Pockets
Pin pattern pieces 1, 2 and 3 to the lining and cut piece 6, pocket, from remaining lining.
The interfacing should be attached to the wrong side of the fur to support it but if you find this too difficult, attach the interfacing to the inner sections of band and pocket tab, rather than omit it completely.
Cut out half pocket tab (this is a band facing), 7, in fur.
Interface, and place fur pieces to fabric pockets.
Stitch across the top taking a 1.5cm (⅝in) seam. Press seam open, trim edges to 1cm (⅜in).

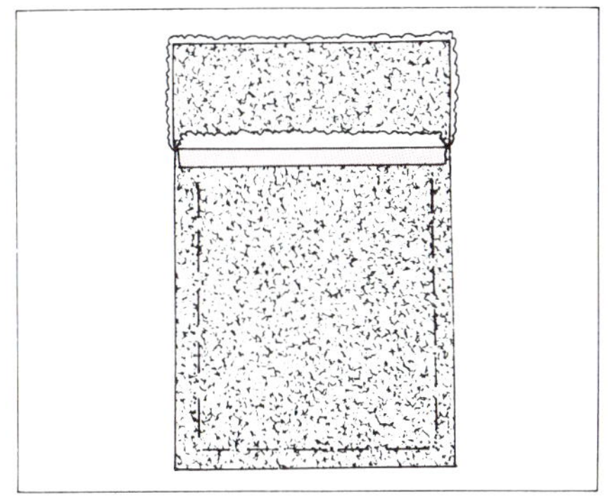

Place fabric tabs to fur edging, right sides together. Machine. Press open the join. Trim edges to 5mm (¼in).

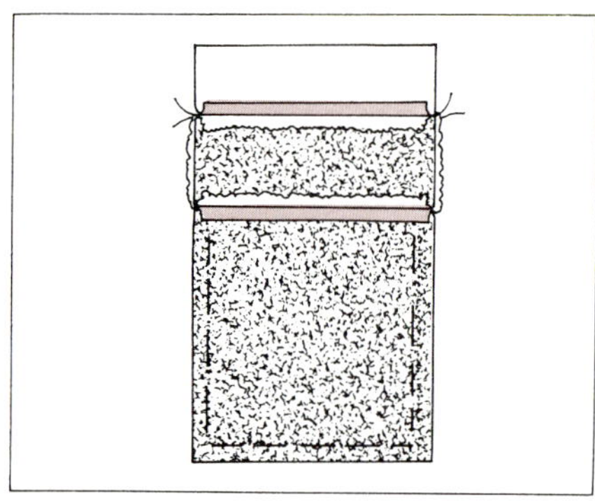

Fold fabric tab over on to fur tab and stitch down the side of the pocket as far as the base of the tab.

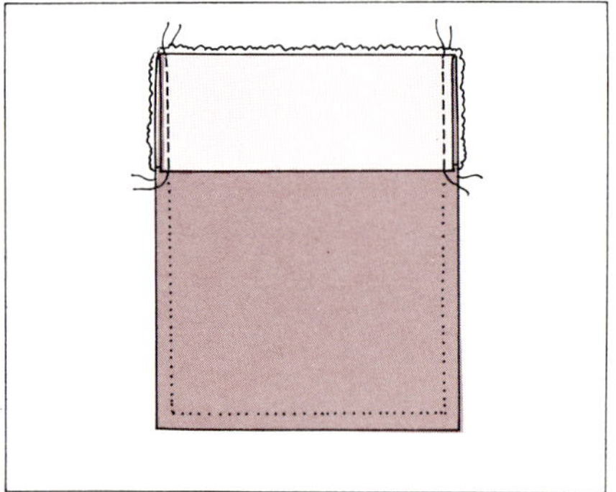

Trim edges as narrow as possible and cut off the corners. Turn tab right side out. Roll the joins to the edge and tack. Baste to hold the two layers together. Turn in the remaining three edges of the pocket and tack close to the edge. Fold the corners into a mitre. Trim off surplus fabric and press well.

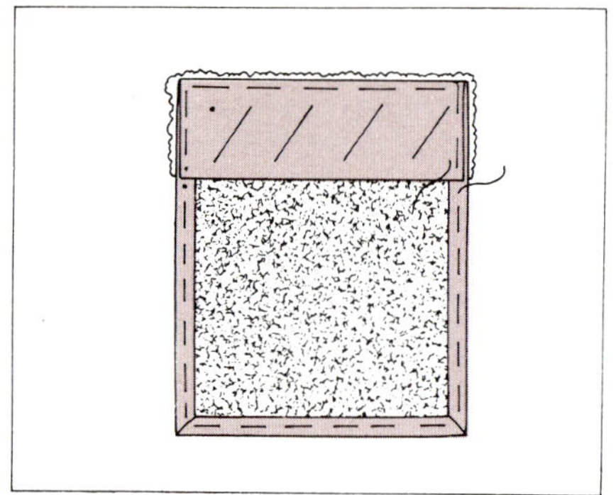

Place lining pieces wrong side down to wrong side of pocket and baste. Trim a little off all edges, turn under so that fold of lining is 2 mm ($\frac{1}{16}$ in) in from the pocket edge and tack. Finish by felling the lining to the pocket. Press.

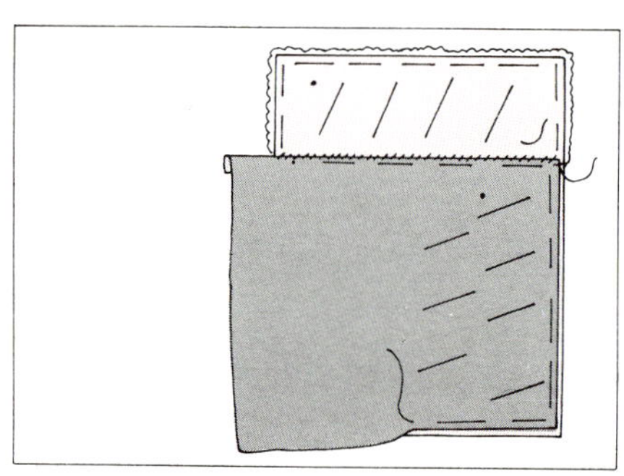

2 Tucks
Tack and machine shoulder tucks, then press.
Tack shoulder seams and side seams.
Fit Slip shoulder pads in and check the fit. Make sure side-seams are vertical. Lift front or back coat at shoulders if adjustment is needed. Take in or let out side seams if necessary and re-fit. Check coat length.
Pin pockets on coat fronts and see if the marked position is comfortable. The edge of the pocket should be about 6 cm ($2\frac{1}{2}$ in) in from the coat edge. Take off coat, mark pocket position and remove pockets.
Make any adjustments to hemline. Remove tacking from shoulder seams, having marked any alterations.

3 Side seams
The coat bands and pocket tabs are 4 cm ($1\frac{1}{2}$ in) wide finished so hem and sleeve bands should be the same.
On the wrong side measure from the coat hem edge 5.5 cm ($2\frac{1}{4}$ in) – the width of the band plus a seam allowance of 1.5 cm ($\frac{5}{8}$ in). Mark this point with chalk. Stitch the coat side seams down as far as the mark. Snip the seam allowance, turn the remaining 5.5 cm ($2\frac{1}{4}$ in) on to the right side, and stitch to the hem.

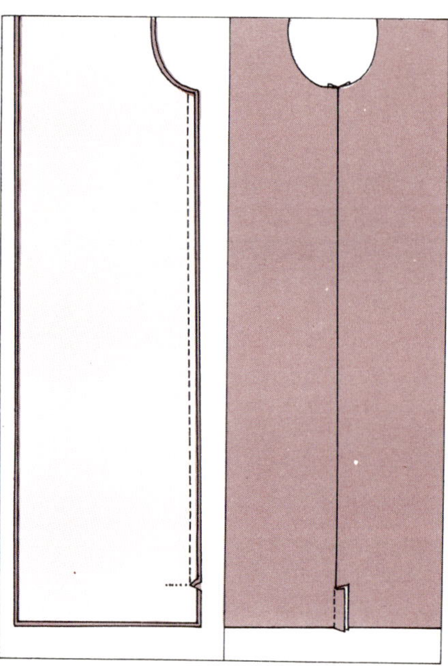

Press open and trim edges to 1 cm ($\frac{3}{8}$ in). Press remainder of coat seam.

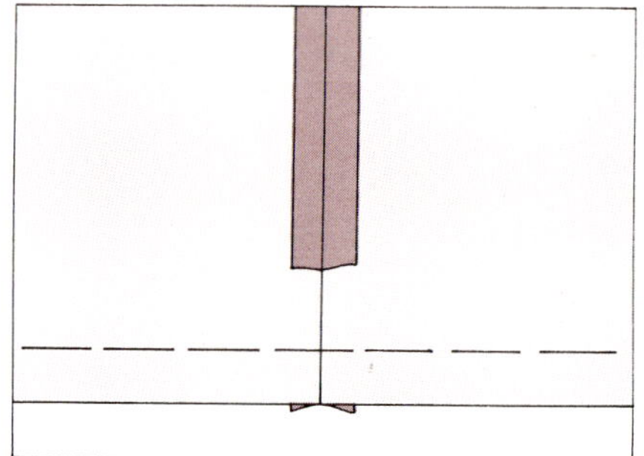

Fold coat so that fronts are together and mark the pocket position using tailor tacks or chalk.
Tack pockets in position on right side of coat, tacking across the top and basting down the middle to hold. Re-tack shoulder seams and try on coat. Stitch pockets in place, using a small catch stitch under the edge and a strong bar tack at the top corners. To stitch the fur tab, turn coat over and back stitch through from the wrong side, catching the pocket firmly. For heavy coat fabrics this is a good way of attaching the entire pocket.

4 Lining
Adjust the length of the pattern pieces so that the lining is 2.5 cm (1 in) shorter than the coat.
Cutting out
Cut out pieces numbered 1, 2 and 3. Place 1 (back) 2.5 cm (1 in) away from the fold instead of on the fold.
Add about 5 mm ($\frac{1}{4}$ in) to all edges. Lining should always be slightly loose within the coat so that it does not pull on the outer fabric. In addition, lining fabrics, with the exception of nylon jersey, have little 'give' and many do not wear very well; any tightness will result in split seams.
Mark the shoulder tucks on the lining using carbon paper. Mark and tack the amount left as a fold in the lining at the centre back. Press the fold to one side. This forms a pleat. The tacking is released when the coat is finished.

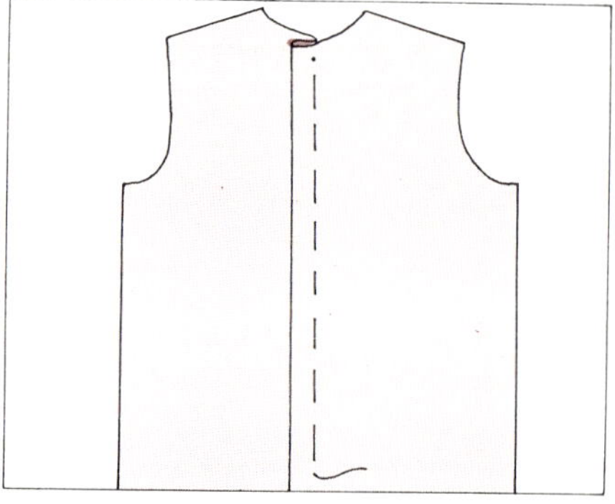

Making up
Stitch shoulder tucks and side seams, making the same adjustments as you made in fitting the coat. Press both lining turnings together towards the front.
Arrange coat wrong side up, place lining on top wrong side down. Match up pleat with coat centre back. Match up side seams. There will be a slight bubbling of lining between these three points; do not smooth it out.
Keeping the coat on the table, baste the lining to the coat starting at the centre back and working up and down in rows almost to the side seams. The stitches should be about 5 cm (2 in) long and the rows can be 5 cm (2 in)

Right: full-length coat (page 14) in herringbone tweed with astrakhan fur trim and matching skirt (page 28), worn with the frilled blouse (page 52) in caramel silk.

Page 18: short jacket (page 13) in grey, red and black check wool; pleated skirt (page 33) in black wool crêpe; blouse (page 48) in white polyester.

13

apart. Do not go too near the neck, armhole or hem edges; they should be left free so that you can still reach them to continue sewing. As you baste, ease the fabric on to the needle but also keep the lining well pushed into the body of the coat; resist the temptation to smooth it out.

On reaching the side seam, fold back the front section of lining, attach the lining turnings to the turning of the coat by working a large half-back stitch through the layers. Slip your fingers under the turnings and stitch from about 10cm (4in) above the hem (this means 10cm (4in) above where the fur will end) to 7cm ($2\frac{3}{4}$in) from the armhole.

Replace the front lining on top of the front coat area, match up the shoulder tucks and continue basting as far as the front edge, but stop about 4cm ($1\frac{1}{2}$in) within the edge (see diagram, top right).

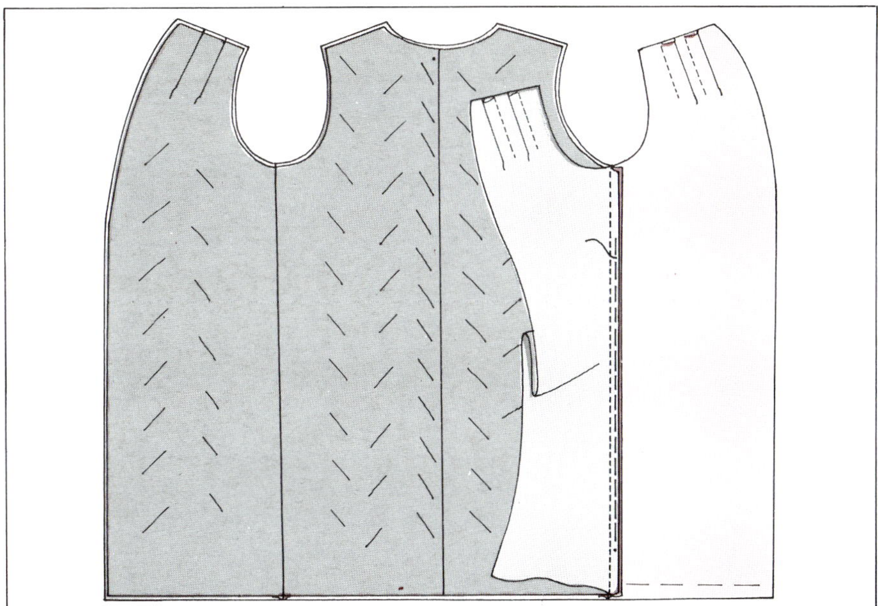

5 Shoulder seams

Outer fabric only: machine then press open.

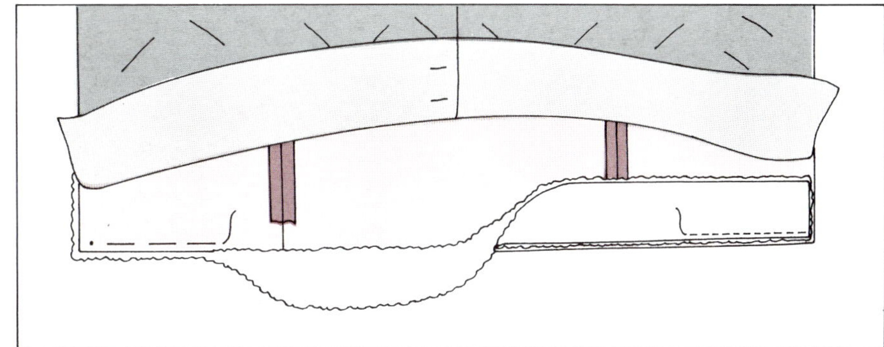

6 Hem

Note When sewing fur, use a large machine stitch. On the right side, ease out any pile that has caught in the seams using the point of a pin. Fur can usually be pressed lightly if placed on a thick towel, but experiment with spare pieces of fur because some fibres may soften and flatten.

Cut a strip of fur 7cm ($2\frac{3}{4}$in) wide and long enough to go round the hem. Place it against the wrong side of the coat, right side down. Tack and machine keeping lining folded back out of the way, taking 1.5cm ($\frac{5}{8}$in) seam allowance and stopping 2.5cm (1in) from the front of the coat. Trim the edges, press open the join and roll the fur to the right side. Tack along the edge, working from the coat side if you find the fur very thick (see diagram right, second from top).

On the right side turn under the edge of the fur evenly. Tack to the coat and hem in place by hand.

7 Bands

Cut out bands in fur and attach interfacing to the wrong side. Join the fur bands and the fabric bands at the centre back. Press open the seam. Trim the edges.

Place fur band to coat, right sides together and matching centre back. Tack and machine keeping lining folded back out of the way. Press the join open, snipping the turnings round the neck so that they lie flat.

Place fabric band to fur, right sides together. Tack and machine outer edge.

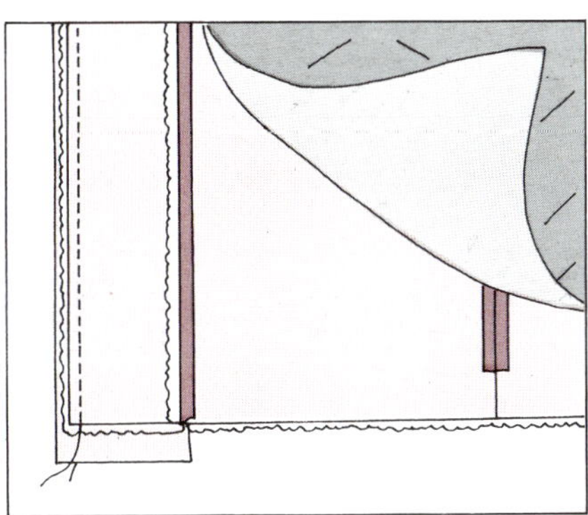

Trim and press open the join. Roll the fabric to the wrong side. Work the join to the edge and tack, again from the fabric side if the fur is difficult to sew.

At the hem turn up the bottom of the band so that it is level with the coat hem. Oversew the edge to hold it.

Tack the raw edge of the band on top of the opened seam beneath. From the right side prick stitch through the seam joining fur to coat. At the hem corners turn in the fur edges to meet each other and hem together. Hem the small gap at the hem where the band meets the fur hem and slip stitch the two edges at the bottom of the band.

Turn coat wrong side up. Turn under and tack lining edge along hem. Turn under edges on top of band fabric too, from hem to armhole. Tack and ease lining back into coat by 2mm ($\frac{1}{16}$in) with each stitch.

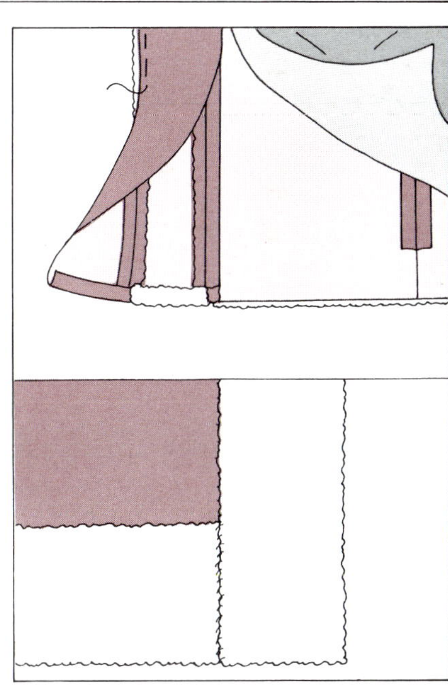

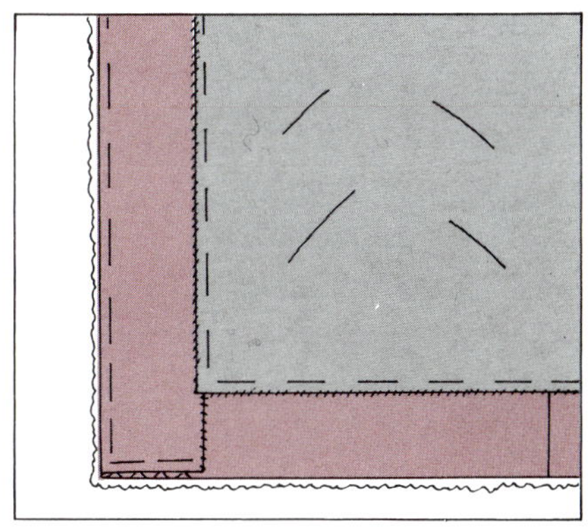

8 Sleeves

Check sleeve length to make sure it is the finished length you need plus 1.5 cm ($\frac{5}{8}$ in). Stitch sleeve seam to 5.5 cm ($2\frac{1}{4}$ in) from the wrist. Snip the turnings and turn the remainder to the right side and stitch. Press open both parts and trim down the raw edges of the lower section.

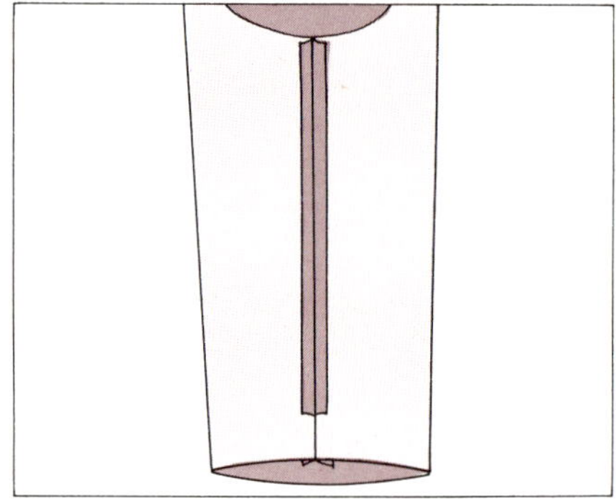

Cut lengths of fur 7 cm ($2\frac{3}{4}$ in) wide and long enough to go round the sleeve plus seam allowances. Tack right side fur to wrong side sleeve, starting and finishing the tacking near the seam. Turn over the two ends of fur to meet each other and slip stitch together by hand. Trim down edges.

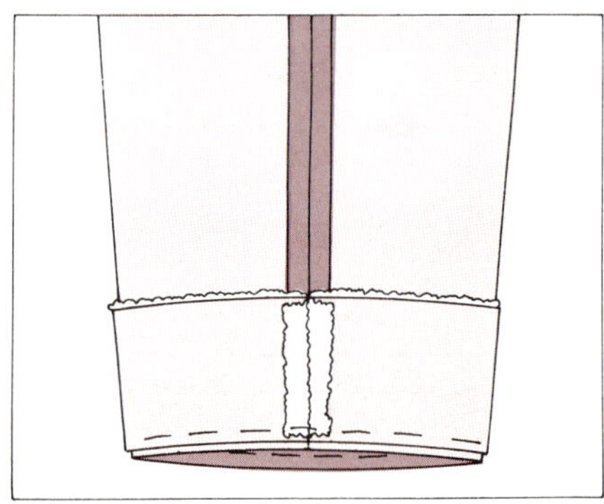

Machine fur to sleeve all round. Press the join open, trim the edges. Roll the fur over to the right side of the sleeve and tack the edge, working from the fabric side for ease. On the right side turn under the edge of the fur, tack to sleeve and hem in place. Press.

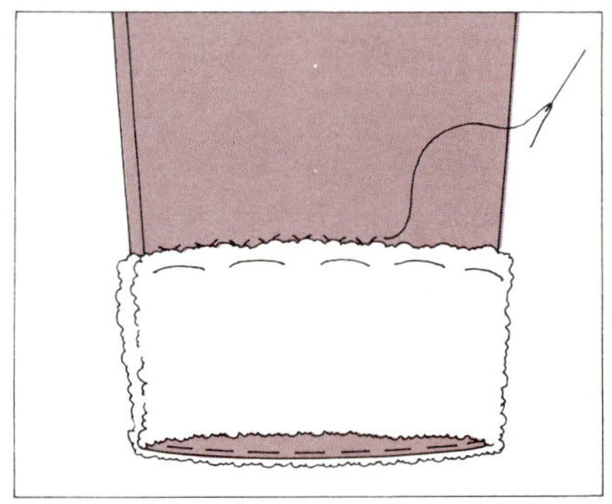

Stitch the seams in the sleeve linings, taking 1.5 cm ($\frac{5}{8}$ in) seam allowances. Press open. Slide lining right side out, over sleeve wrong side out, and match up the seams. Hold the seam allowances together with back stitches for 6 cm ($2\frac{1}{4}$ in) at the middle of the seam. Smooth lining over sleeve and work 3 or 4 rows of basting up and down the sleeve but leave the hem and sleeve head free and also leave in the bubbles of ease that appear.

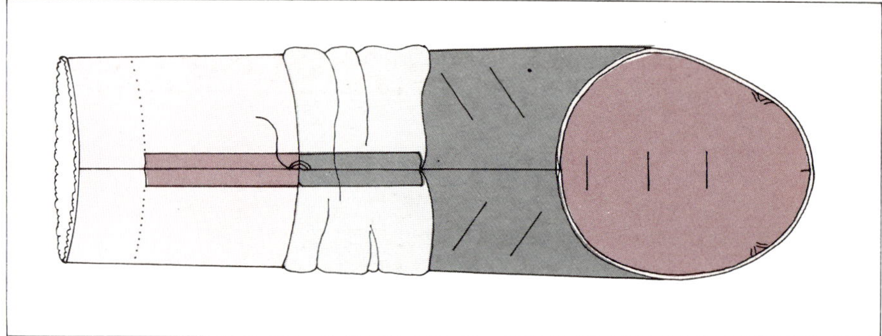

At the hem turn under the lining and tack to the sleeve 2.5 cm (1 in) from the bottom. Fell round to finish.

Set sleeves into armholes holding the lining clear of the stitching.

9 Hanging loop

Make a length of rouleau from lining and tack it to the back neck of the coat over the edge of the band.

10 Finishing

Insert the shoulder pads and sleeve head roll (see right) to make the sleeve hang well.

At the shoulders, tack the back lining flat over the shoulder seam and pad. Back stitch in place.

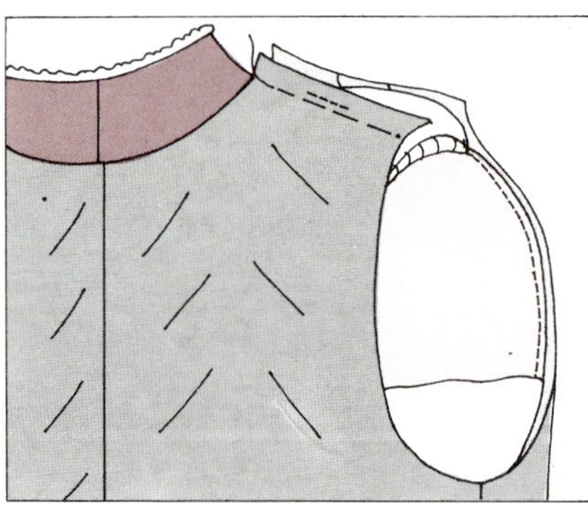

Turn under the edge of the front lining and allow it to cover the back lining along the shoulder line. Turn in and tack remaining raw edge round neckline, easing the lining back. Complete the armhole by trimming a little from the raw edges of the armhole. Bring garment lining over armhole and back stitch the turnings to the garment turnings. Bring edge of sleeve lining up over the garment armhole, turn in the edge and pin at intervals. The ease in the sleeve head will appear as bulges between the pins. The sleeve lining should cover the back stitches. Tack. Complete by felling all lining edges including armholes, shoulders, hem and front edges. Remove tackings. If the lining needs pressing use a cool iron, supporting sleeve with pad or towel.

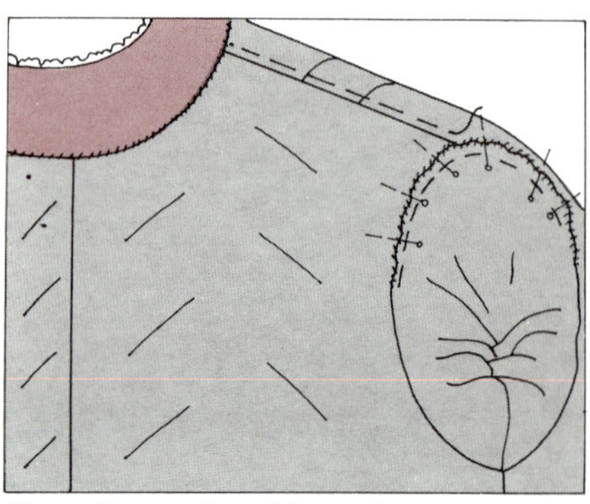

Press the coat and hang it up to cool.

Sleeve head roll

The hang of a coat or jacket is improved by the addition of a sleeve head roll at the armhole edge of the shoulder pad. The roll supports the sleeve head in wear and reduces creasing and limpness. Insert pads then cut a length of wadding (polyester for washable garments) equal in length to the edge of the shoulder pad. Make the roll about 7 cm ($2\frac{3}{4}$ in) in circumference at the centre but tapering to nothing at each end. Place the roll beside the shoulder pad and attach it with loose oversewing stitches that pass right over the roll and into the edge of the armhole turnings and shoulder pad.

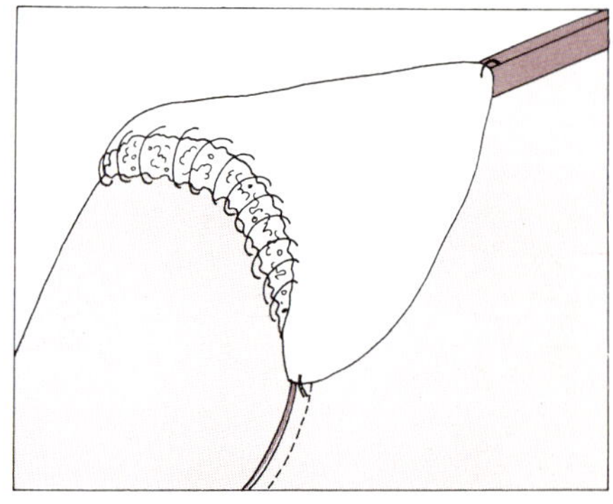

If the coat is lined, the shoulder assembly will be covered by the lining but it is still important to anchor it permanently at this stage. If it is not lined cover the roll with lining before attaching.

LONG JACKET

An unlined evening coat made up using the basic pattern cut to three-quarter length. We made it in brocade to go with the camisole (page 68) in embossed silk and the trousers (page 60) in black French jersey.

FABRIC

Use plain or patterned, crisp or sheer fabrics, including brocade, satin, crêpe, chiffon, georgette, moracain, velvet, panné velvet, printed wool, voile, crêpe de chine, embroidered or embossed fabrics.

Quantities

Refer to the quantities needed for the full length coat on page 15.
This version is 31 cm (12 in) shorter so it takes a little less fabric.
Interfacing is needed for back neck and front edges. Use light iron-on or sew-in interfacing. With sheer fabrics omit interfacing and finish with a rolled edge or machining instead of using the facings.
Finished length back neck to hem: 84 cm (33 in).

HABERDASHERY

- 2 reels thread
- Interfacing (see above)
- Adhesive web
- Fine machine needle if you are using fine fabric e.g. 70(9) for crêpe de chine or chiffon

PATTERN PIECES

1, 2 and 4 to line marked View C on pattern; 3 and 5.

CUTTING OUT

As for basic jacket, page 8.

MAKING UP

Make up as the basic jacket (page 9), omitting pockets. Omit shoulder pads; but lift shoulders to compensate, at the first fitting.

Techniques for use on sheer fabrics
Surplus seam allowance should be trimmed off after fitting but before working any of the following:

Narrow seam
Place fabric pieces right side together. Tack on seam line and machine. Remove tacks. Press the stitching. Trim the raw edges to 3mm ($\frac{1}{8}$in) or a little more on fabrics that are loosely woven or inclined to stretch.
Neaten the raw edges by machine. Use a stitch that is a combination of straight and zig-zag as this produces a softer finish than zig-zag only.
If your machine does a combination stitch such as overlocking, use this to make the seam, omitting the first row of straight stitching. Press seams flat.
Neck, front edges, hems and sleeves can be finished with a rolled or a zig-zag edge.

Rolled edge
This can be worked by hand, or with the hemming foot attached to the machine adjusted to small straight or zig-zag stitch. Preliminary practice on a long spare piece of fabric is essential.
To hand hem, hold the fabric wrong side towards you and fold the raw edge over twice. Each fold should be as narrow as the fabric will allow. It often helps to moisten the finger tips of the left hand. Now roll and hold the edge while hemming with the other hand.

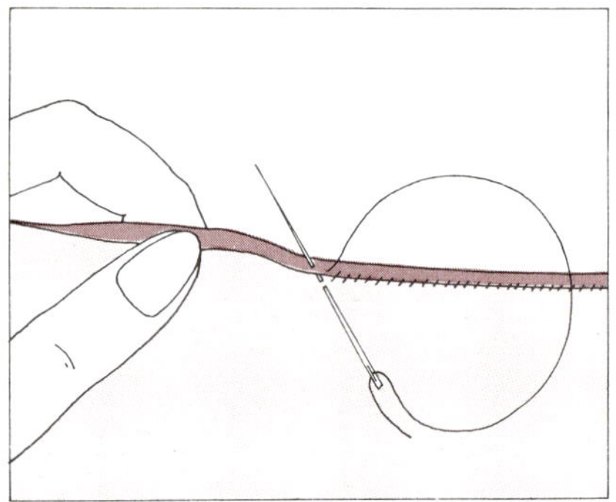

Do not tack. Work close hemming or slip-hemming picking up only one thread to prevent the stitches from showing on the outside. Press to finish.

Zig-zag edge
Fold under 5mm ($\frac{1}{4}$in), tack and press, trim away the bulk e.g. on coat shoulder and side seams. Do not tack too near the fold.
Set the machine to a very small zig-zag – almost satin stitch, or use a small decorative stitch. Machine the edge right side up. When the needle moves to the right it should just clear the fold.
Press the stitching. On the wrong side trim off the raw edge close to the machining.

BELTED COAT OR ROBE

A coat length version of the pattern with tie belt, bands and pockets. This can be made in a variety of formal or casual fabrics to make anything from a raincoat to a robe.
We made it up in the largest size (18) for a man, using black paisley façonné.

FABRIC

We made the coat in showerproof polyester cotton gaberdine and the robe in paisley façonné. You could use wool, brocade, towelling, tweed, flannel, bouclé, velveteen, moiré taffeta or crêpe.
We lined the coat version with a matching check viyella.

Quantities
The same as for the coat (see page 15).
Interfacing is needed for bands, belt, pockets. Use light or medium iron-on or sew-in interfacing.
If making a robe, omit shoulder pads and lift shoulders at fitting (see page 9) to compensate.
If making up the pattern for a man, lengthen the front, back, sleeve and belt as required (also band pattern) and buy sufficient extra fabric.
The coat may be lined. Buy the same quantity of lining as fabric and follow instructions for lining edge to edge coat version (page 16).
Finished length back neck to hem: 113cm ($44\frac{1}{2}$in).

HABERDASHERY

2 reels thread
Interfacing (as above)
1 pair shoulder pads
A small piece of lining (omit if making a robe)

PATTERN PIECES

1, 2, 3, 6, 7, 9 and 10.

CUTTING OUT

Follow cutting lines for View D on the pattern.
Cut out 7, 9, 10 in interfacing.
Pin all pattern pieces to fabric following layout diagram and cut out 1, 2, 3 and 10, leaving the others until required.
When ready, open out remaining fabric and press the interfacing pieces of 7, 9, 10 to the wrong side. Cut out.
Cut out a second pair of bands in fabric.
Note the seam allowance on the belt is 1cm ($\frac{3}{8}$in).

Marking
Mark tucks, armhole and sleeve head points, balance marks on band and coat edge. Mark centre back fold of coat.

MAKING UP

1 Belt
Attach light iron-on interfacing to wrong side of belt. Fold in half, right sides together, and tack across the ends and along belt keeping the tacking fairly close to the raw edges. Press very lightly to flatten. Rule a chalk line on which to stitch. Mark both sides of belt. Midway along the belt mark off with chalk a distance of about 7cm ($2\frac{3}{4}$in) to leave as a gap for turning the belt. Mark gap on both sides.
Stitch across one end and along the belt, stopping at the gap; fasten off stitching. Turn belt over, machine second side, stitching across the end and along to the gap. This method prevents movement of fabric.

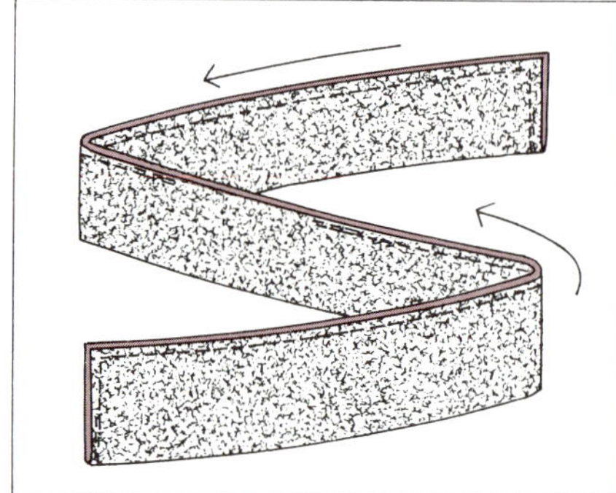

Trim edges, cut off surplus fabric at corners. Press stitching. Use a ruler or knitting needle and turn belt right side out by pushing the ends inwards and pulling out at the gap.
Roll one edge so that seam is exactly on the edge of the belt and tack. Ease out the corners to make a square end. At this gap turn in the raw edges and tack together. Press belt. Slip stitch the gap to close it. Work top stitching round belt if you wish.

2 Tucks
Fold coat fronts wrong side out and match up tuck markings. Tack and machine tucks. Press towards neck.

3 Shoulder and side seams
Place coat fronts to coat back, right sides together, matching edges. Tack, taking 1.5cm ($\frac{5}{8}$in) seam allowance. Fit, checking the points listed for the basic jacket. Then tie the belt round the waist. Pin the interfaced pocket pieces to the coat front, adjusting it to establish a good position. Remember that because this coat wraps over, the pockets will have to be moved closer to the side seams than in the unbelted versions. Also, at this fitting turn up and pin the hem. Mark hem length and pocket position with chalk and remove pins.
Machine and press the seams, using open seams.
Turn up and tack the coat hem at the level pinned, tacking the fold and again above to hold the hem surplus.
Put the coat on, tie the belt, and check the length. Adjust and re-tack if necessary.
Mark the hem line with tailor's chalk or pins and then remove the tacking to let the hem down in order to attach the bands.
Check that the front edges are equal by folding coat in half at centre back.

4 Bands
One pair of bands should be interfaced. Join at the centre back and press open the joins. Join the other two band facing pieces and press.
Trim the joins and cut off the corners to reduce bulk.

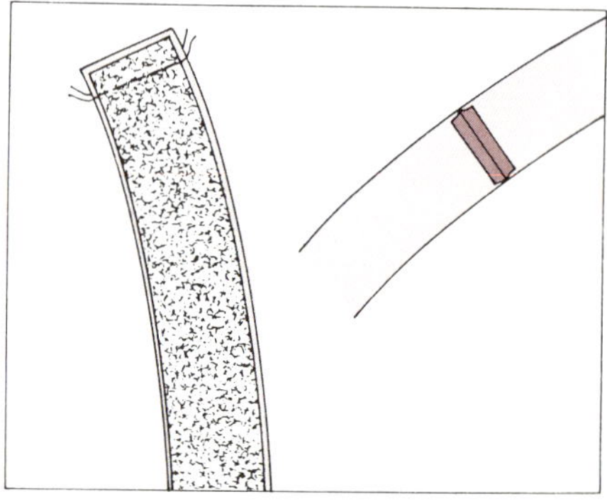

Place interfaced bands to coat, matching seam of band to centre back of coat, pin. Holding raw edges together, tack from the centre back round the neck and down to the hem of the coat, matching the balance marks. Turn coat round and return to neck and tack the other side.

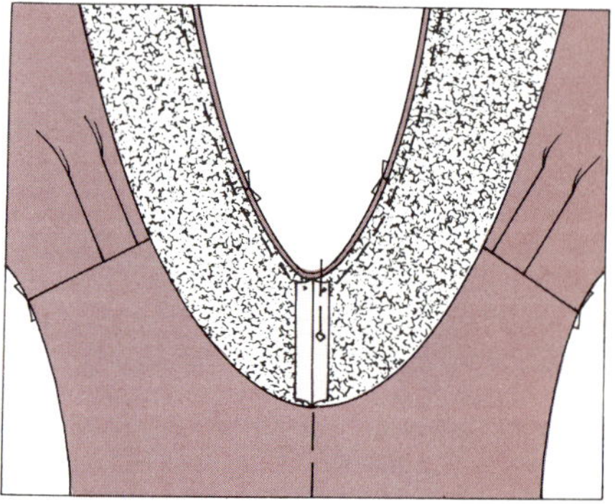

Machine band to coat, again stitching in two parts, starting at the centre back each time. Remove tackings; press seam open and trim the turnings to 5mm ($\frac{1}{4}$in) or less. Snip the turnings at neck curves. On light fabric press both turnings towards the band, on medium and heavy ones leave the seam open.
Place the second pair of bands right side down to right side of coat, with edges and back neck seams matching.

Insert a pin to hold seams together. Tack and machine from centre back round to the hem. Press the join open.

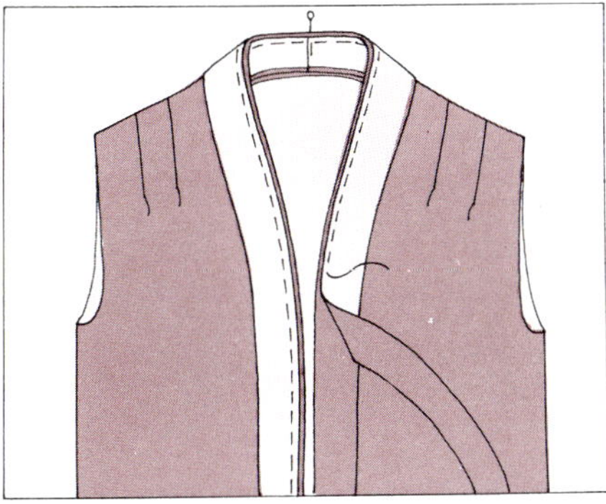

Trim and snip the raw edges and layer them. Work out the edge and roll it until the join is at the edge, then work from right side and tack with the join slightly out of sight.
Turn up the coat hem for a distance of about 20cm (8in) including band. Tack the hem fold. Trim down the surplus within the band.

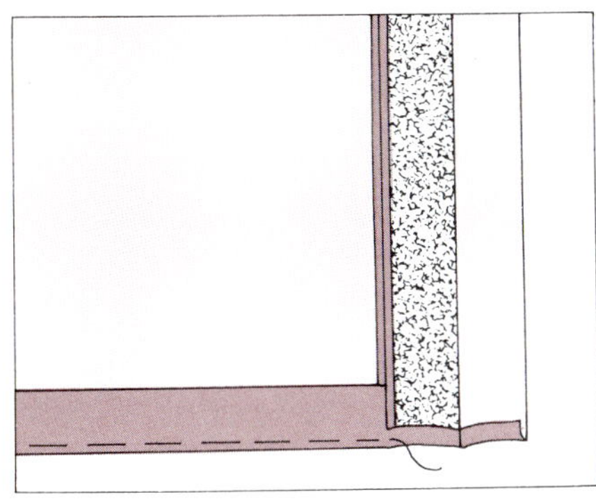

Fold over the band facing piece and tack the bottom corner. Baste the band to the band facing right round the coat.
Arrange the coat right side out, check that the two front edges are equal from back neck to hem. Turn up and tack the remainder of the coat hem.

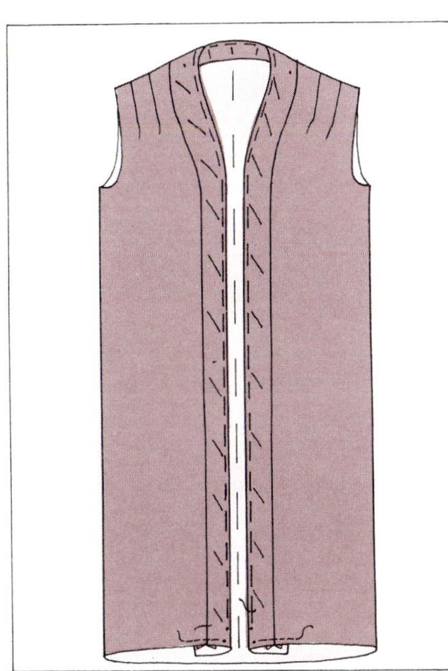

Trim the hemline evenly and neaten with overcasting or zig-zag.
On the inside, finish the band facing edge. On thick fabrics neaten the edge and then work prick stitch by hand in the join keeping the seam open. Slip stitch at the hem.
Remove basting and press. Leave the edge tacking in place until the coat is complete.
On finer fabric trim a little off the facing edge, turn it under and tack it down. Press, then hem into the machining. Slip stitch the folds at the hem. Leave in the edge tacking but remove all other tacks.

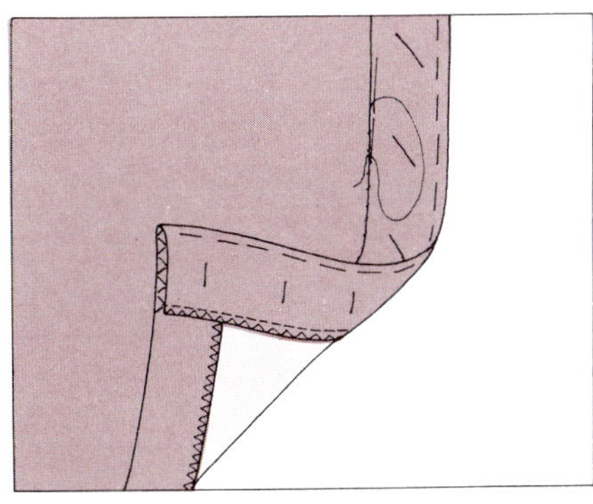

Complete the remainder of the coat hem as for basic jacket. On a casual robe the hem and the sleeve hems could be machined.

5 Pockets

Interface pocket tab (band facing) only for a casual robe; interface tab and pocket for coats made in soft fabrics; for lined coats interface both pieces and also line the larger piece of pocket.
Mark exact size of pocket on interfacing using tracing wheel and carbon paper and mark fold line on tab.
Place pocket tab to pocket, right sides facing, and machine across the top on the seam line. Press join open, trim edges to 5mm ($\frac{1}{4}$in). On light or fraying fabrics press both turnings up towards tab.
Neaten edge of pocket tab, including the interfacing.
Turn in remaining edges of pocket on seam line and tack. Trim away the ends of the tab seam to reduce bulk and mitre the pocket corners, folding the fabric at an angle and trimming away bulk underneath. Tack, press.
Fold over tab on fold line and tack and press. Hold down either by working a row of prick stitch in the join or a row of machining. On fine fabrics, turn under the tab edge, tack down on to machine stitches and hem into machining.
Slip stitch the tab ends.
To line pocket cut lining pieces 1cm ($\frac{3}{8}$in) smaller than the main pocket piece, place wrong side down to wrong side of pocket and attach by basting.
Turn under raw edge of lining so that it covers the tab edge. Tack. Turn in the other three edges so that they are 2mm ($\frac{1}{16}$in) in from the pocket edges. Tack and press. Hem or fell the lining to the pocket.
On the right coat front draw a clear chalk line indicating exactly where the pocket top is to go. Fold coat so that the two sides match exactly. Bang sharply on the pocket area to transfer the chalk. Open out coat, place pockets on chalk marks and tack along the top. Baste down the centre to hold in position. Try on. Adjust if necessary.
Tack pocket all round edges. Attach by working a small slip stitch under the edge and a bartack 2mm ($\frac{1}{16}$in) in from the top corners. On casual coats, the pockets can be machined in place.

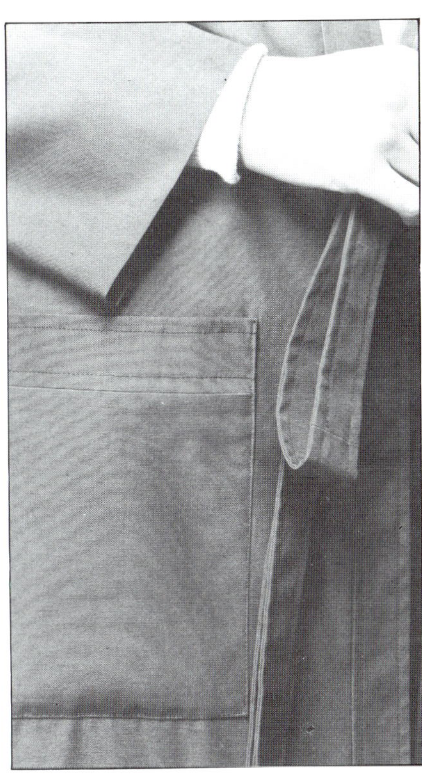

FULL-LENGTH ROBE

A full-length robe with bands, belt and pockets in the side seams. The sleeves can have bands added. This can be made as a utility or a luxury robe. We used dark green velvet.

FABRIC

For a utility version you could use velour, towelling, quilting, cotton, or brushed viscose. For a luxury robe choose from satin, silk, light wool, lace, velvet or voile.

Quantities
You will need to add at least 35cm (14in) to the length of the coat pattern. Pin on an extra piece of paper and extend all edges by an equal amount using a ruler. Draw in a new hemline. Lengthen the bands in the same way by the same amount. Size 12 will take about 1 metre extra of 90cm (36in) fabric, or about 80cm extra of 150cm (60in) fabric. Interfacing is needed for pockets. With heavier fabrics, cut pocket linings too. Robes are not usually interfaced.

HABERDASHERY

2 reels thread

Small piece adhesive web

PATTERN PIECES

1, 2, 3, 9, 10 and 14 (skirt pocket).

CUTTING OUT

Cut out piece 14 in interfacing. Cut 1, 2, 3, 9, 10.
Open out remaining fabric, press interfacing s 14 to wrong side and cut out.
Note If you like big pockets, enlarge them when cutting.

Marking
As for coat version, page 24.

MAKING UP

1 Tucks, hanging loop and belt loops
Machine and press tucks. Top stitch on the right side to finish. Make a length of tubing 32 cm (13 in) long for a hanging loop and for belt loops. Cut off 8 cm (3 in) and tack on wrong side of the back at the neckline. Cut the remainder in two, fold each piece double and tack at the side seam edge at waist level on the right side of the back robe section.

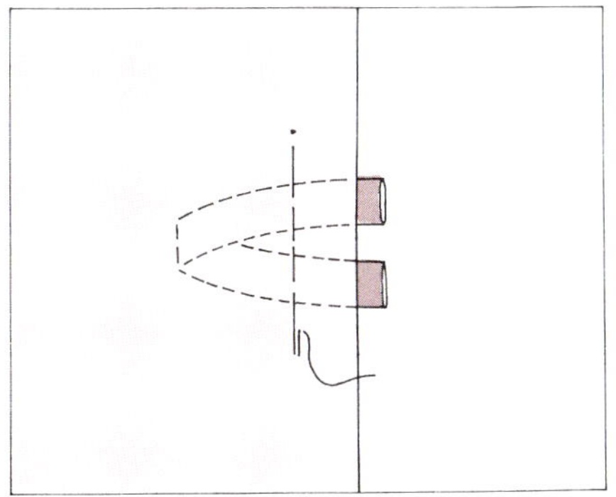

2 Shoulder seams, side seams and pockets
Tack shoulder and side seams. Decide on a suitable level for the pockets and mark the top with chalk on right and wrong sides. Mark pocket bottoms 17 cm ($6\frac{1}{2}$ in) below. Try on robe. Stitch, neaten and press open shoulder and side seams as marked. Slip a narrow piece of adhesive web under the front seam allowance where the pocket gap comes and press. Machine stitching can be added to match shoulder tucks.
Place pocket piece right side down on the seam, matching the straight edge to the edge of the seam allowance. Machine together taking the smallest possible seam allowance.
Baste pocket flat to robe and tack round the curved edge just inside the neatening on the right side. Work a row of machining beside the tacking to hold the pocket in position.

3 Belt and hem
Make belt as described for previous coat, but omitting interfacing.
Turn up hem to correct level. Tack and press the fold. Trim the surplus evenly, leaving as much as possible to weight the robe. Neaten and finish with adhesive web, hand catch stitch or a row of machining.

4 Bands
Join each pair of bands at the centre back. Press open and trim the edges. Place both bands right sides together and seams together. Tack along the outer edge. Machine.
Trim turnings to 5 mm ($\frac{1}{4}$ in) or less.
Press the join open, then roll the bands right side out. Tack and press. Work a row of basting along the middle from end to end to keep both layers together.
Place made up band to right side of robe, matching seam to centre back. Tack band to robe edge down to hem. As you reach the hem, open the bands, turn up the end so that the band is level with robe hem. Trim off surplus band to 1 cm ($\frac{3}{8}$ in), refold the band and tack to robe. Machine band to robe. Trim the raw edges and neaten them all together. Press band to extend beyond edge of robe.

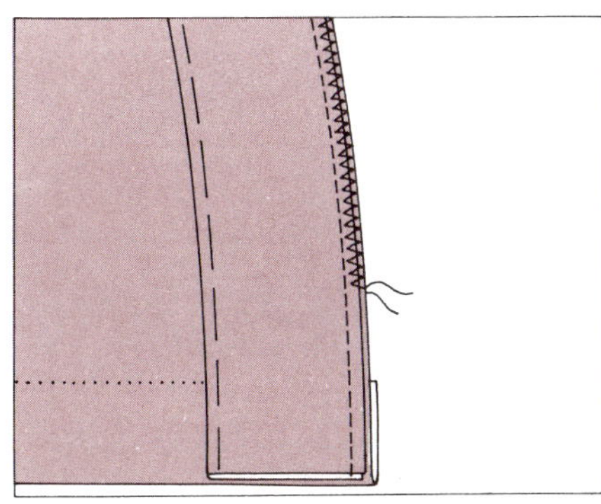

The band can be machined at the outer edge and also a row of machining can be worked beside the join, through robe and trimmings.

Attaching the bands has stitched the hanging loop in place.

5 Sleeves
Cut two pieces of fabric, preferably on the cross, for sleeve bands 17 cm ($6\frac{1}{2}$ in) deep and exactly the width of the sleeve. Stitch sleeve seams and neaten. Fold the bands and join the ends. Trim the edges and press open.

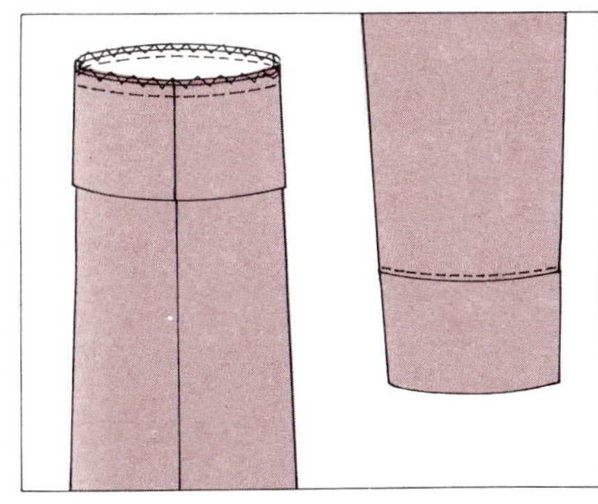

Fold bands wrong sides together and baste. Press.
Neaten sleeve and band edges.
Slip band over the sleeve on the right side with seams matching.
Tack. Machine band to sleeve. Press band to extend. Work a row of machining beside the join to hold the seam edge down.
Set sleeves into armholes and neaten.

SKIRT

A classic shaped skirt, hem finishing on the knee with panelled front, shaping the skirt into the waist. The back is fitted with darts and a side zip. Pockets are inserted in the front panel to keep a slim line. We made it in grey flannel to match the jacket (page 7).

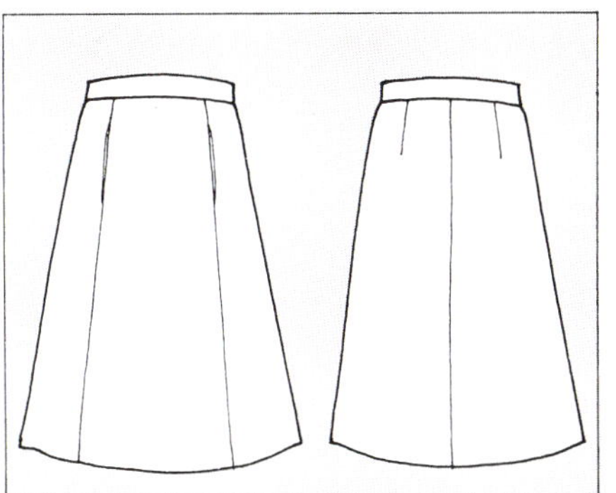

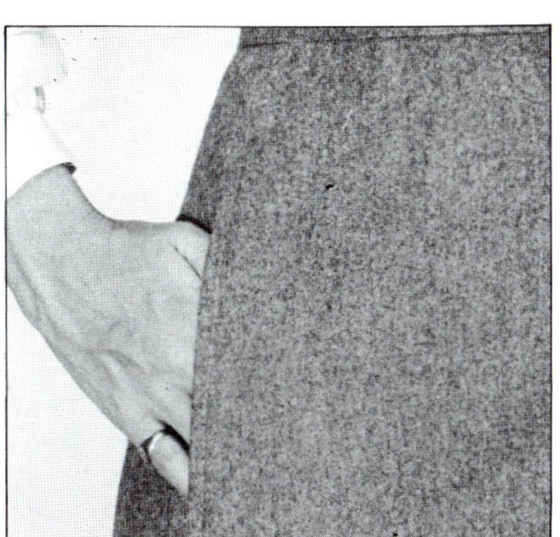

Fold fabric wrong sides together

115 cm (45 in) fabric

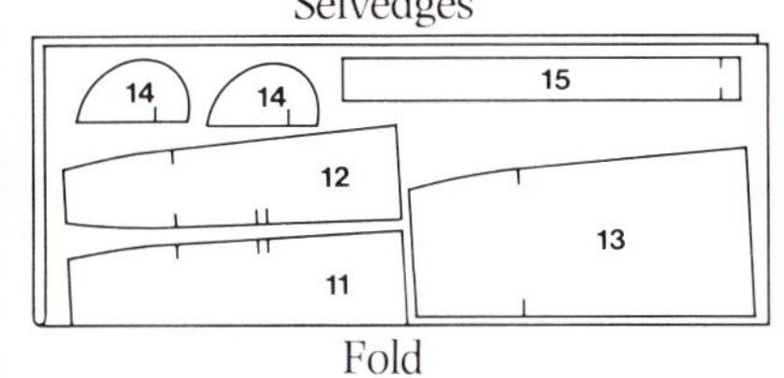

Cut piece 15 from single layer of fabric only

140 cm (54 in) fabric

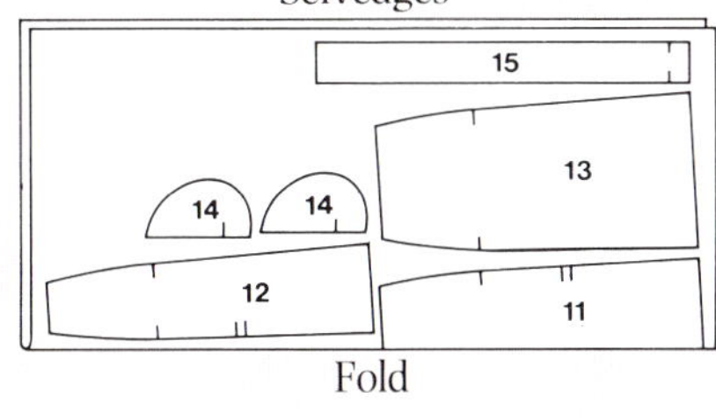

Cut piece 15 from single layer of fabric only

150 cm (60 in) fabric

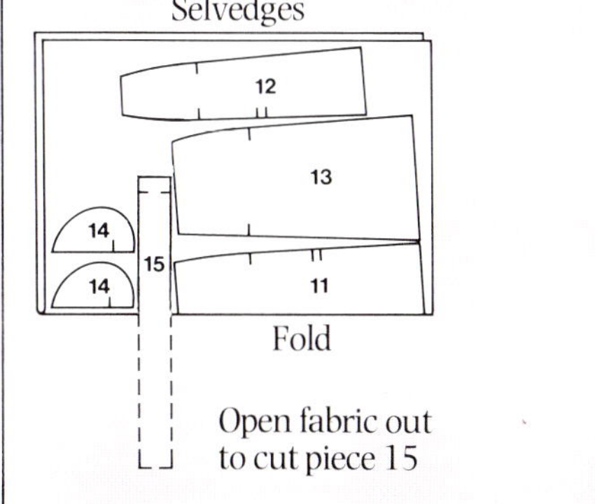

Open fabric out to cut piece 15

FABRIC

Any of the jacket fabrics, page 8 as well as jersey, tweed or suede.

Quantities

Width	*Size*	*Quantity*
115cm (45in)	10	1.50m
	12	1.50m
	14	1.50m
	16	1.55m
	18	1.55m
140cm (54in)	As for 115cm	
150cm (60in)	10	1.10m
	12	1.10m
	14	1.10m
	16	1.15m
	18	1.15m

Lining You will need the same quantity of lining as fabric.
Finished length (not including waistband): 64.5cm ($25\frac{1}{2}$in).

HABERDASHERY

- 2 reels thread
- Iron-on interfacing for pockets
- Length of perforated, iron-on waistband interfacing
- 20cm (8in) metal or nylon zip or 23cm (9in) if you have large hips
- Waistband fastening: a button, a large trouser hook or a strip of Velcro
- Petersham or straight seam binding

PATTERN PIECES

11, 12, 13, 14 and 15.

CUTTING OUT

Cut out 14 (pocket) in iron-on interfacing.
Pin pattern pieces 11, 12 and 13 to fabric following layout.
Pin 15 and 14 in place.
Cut out 11, 12, 13 and leave the rest until required.

Marking

Mark centre front fold, back darts, balance marks on centre back seam, centre front panel and side front panel: the single one indicates the pocket position. Mark the zip point mark on the side seam.

MAKING UP

1 Darts and back seam

Place the two skirt back pieces right sides together with centre back edges together and balance marks matching. Tack from hem to waist taking 1.5cm ($\frac{5}{8}$in) seam allowance. Make a short chalk mark at the left side edge on the zip point, on the wrong side of the fabric.
(Diagram, above right.)
Fold each back section wrong side out and match up the dart markings. (If the darts have been marked with tailor's tacks you can feel both sets and line them up.) Tack.
(Diagram right.)

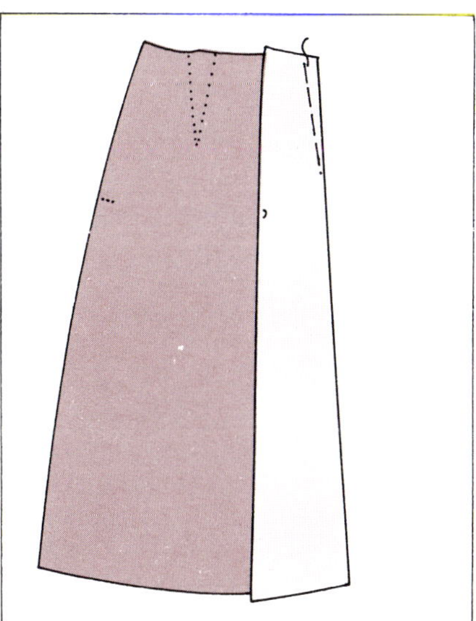

Now tack panel seams to centre front from hem to waist, matching balance marks and including the part where the pocket will be.

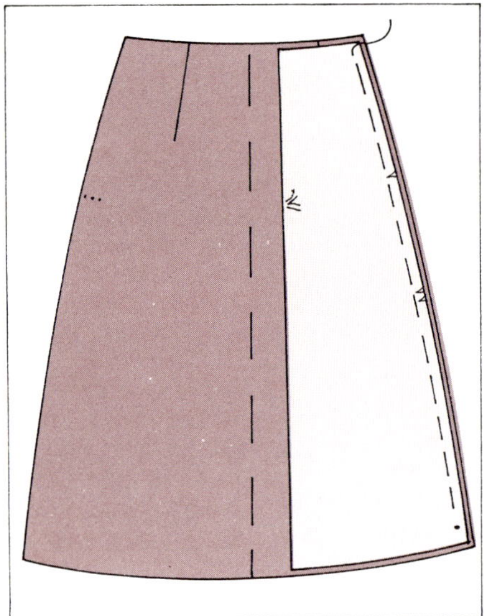

Open out skirt front, place back skirt on top, matching side seams, edges and balance marks. Tack side seams from hem to waist. Tack the left seam only as far as the zip point.

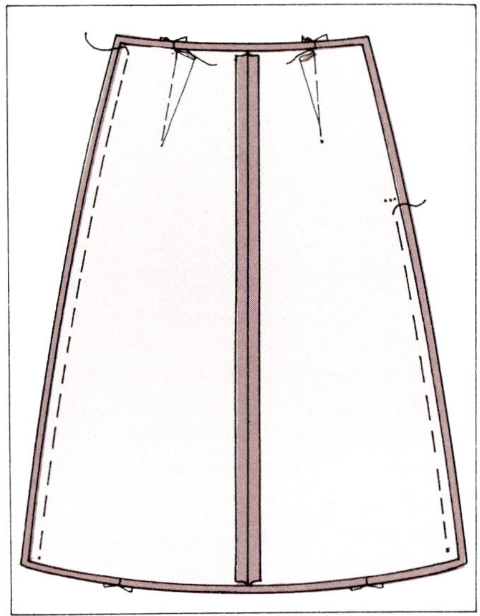

Fit Put skirt on, pin up side opening and check the darts panel seams and centre back seam.
The darts should produce an area of fullness over the buttocks. Adjust if necessary by lengthening or shortening darts. A figure with a flat seat will need a narrower dart; reduce width at the waist for less fullness at the point.

2 Panel seams
These are easy to fit with the pocket areas tacked up. The seams should run smoothly over the stomach area and straight to the hem. A thigh bulge on the front of the legs will produce a lateral crease so release the seams from above thigh level and let them out. Remember that the pockets will add bulk. They can be left out altogether for a flatter fit.

To let out the seams, snip the tacking and re-pin. If the waist is too big, pin a little more out of the panel seam.
The centre back seam should hang straight. If the back waist is too big or if you have a hollow back (the two often go together), snip the tacking and take in the seam at the waist.
If extensive adjustments are needed in all the above positions it is easier to take off the skirt and put it on inside out to insert the pins more accurately.
Remove tacking from side seams.
Mark all alterations with tailor's chalk on the wrong side and remove all pins.
Re-tack and try on again.
Stitch the darts, beginning at the waist edge. Run the stitching gradually into the fold of the fabric at the point of the dart. The final stitch should fall exactly on the fold. Reverse along the fold to fasten off the stitch.

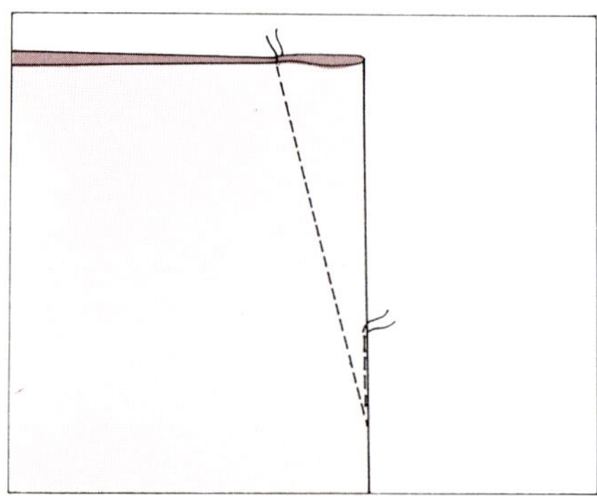

Press the stitching flat then place dart wrong side up on sleeve board or pressing pad. Press the bulk of the dart towards the centre back seam of the garment. Press lightly at first, turn the fabric over and check the right side, then press again more firmly. Press the right side lightly.
If the fabric is bulky, trim the folded edge away and cut the edges to different widths. If the fabric frays, neaten the raw edges.
A further way of reducing bulk in heavy fabrics is to trim the dart and press it open.

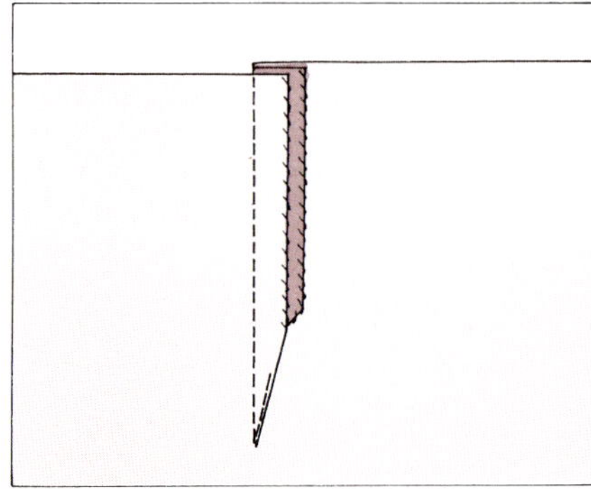

Machine, press open and neaten the back seam.

3 Pockets
Cut out 1 pair of pocket sections from fabric, mark the single balance mark.
Pin skirt pattern pieces 11, 12, 13 to lining, following layout diagram. Press the pocket interfacing pieces to the wrong side of a spare piece of lining and cut round. Mark the single balance mark on the edge.
Remove tacking from panel seams on skirt front.
Place fabric pocket pieces to side panel sections of skirt right side down, matching the balance marks. Place the interfaced pocket pieces right side down on centre panel matching in the same way. Tack and machine in position from top of pocket to balance mark, taking 5 mm ($\frac{1}{4}$ in) seam allowance.

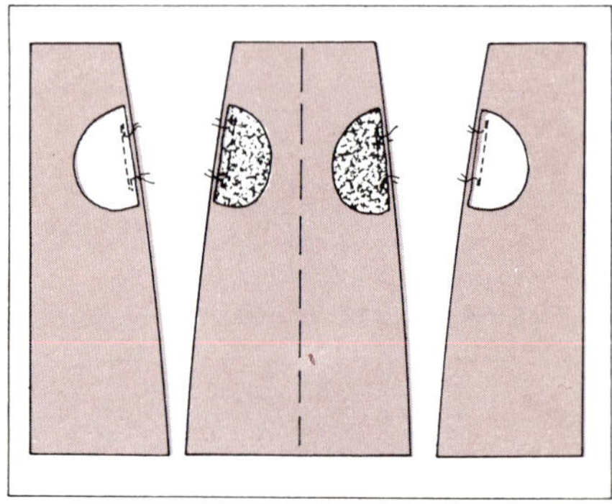

Press all pocket seams open.
Place side panels on centre panel of skirt, right sides together with pockets and seam edges matching. Pin across pocket then tack seam from hem to waist. Machine the panel seam from the pocket balance mark to the hem and from pocket top to waist. On these seams take 1.5 cm ($\frac{5}{8}$ in) seam. As a smaller seam was taken when attaching the pockets to prevent the joins showing on the outside of the skirt, the machine stitching will not join up. Compensate for this by overlapping by about 1 cm ($\frac{3}{8}$ in).

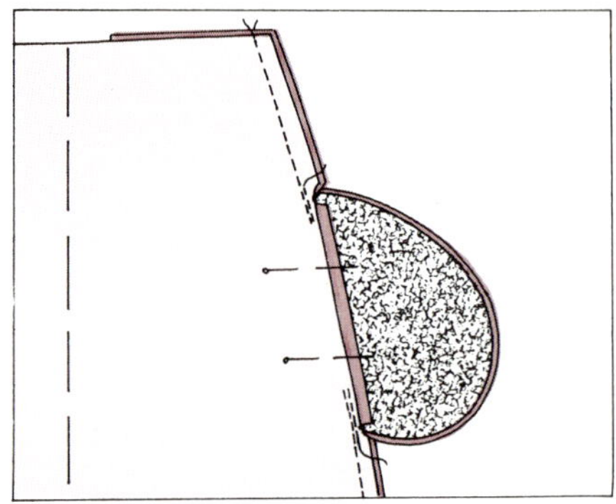

Neaten the raw edges of the seams including the part where the pocket is attached. Remove tackings. Press seams open. Turn skirt right side up and press the seams on wrong side. Press again so both pocket pieces face towards centre of skirt. The pocket should not be obvious. The seam should be smooth and even on the

right side. After pressing, tack pocket edge flat.
On the wrong side baste the two pieces of pocket bag together and draw a curved chalk line for machining.
Stitch from skirt seam round the bag through both layers, turn the corner and stitch up as far as the balance mark. Trim the raw edges to within 5mm ($\frac{1}{4}$in) of the stitching and zig-zag or overcast them together to neaten.
When skirt is complete remove the tackings in the pocket opening.
To prevent the pocket dropping out of position in wear, place a length of seam binding between the waist edge of the skirt and the pocket bag. Turn under and hem the end to attach to pocket bag. Tack the other end to the waist edge. It will be included in the waist finish later to hold it permanently.

4 Side seams
Place back and front skirt sections right sides together and tack side seams.
Turn under and tack the seam allowance on the front edge above the zip point. Tack the side seams a second time for strength, from the right side, with both turnings towards the front.
Fit Put on the skirt and pin up the opening. Look at the side seams and check the fit over waist, hips and thighs.
The seams should hang vertically. If they do not, lift either back or front waist of skirt to correct. If there is tightness or excess fabric over the hips or thighs, snip the tacking and pin the adjustment. Also check the width of the skirt at the hem.
Pass a length of waistband interfacing round your waist over the skirt and pin the ends. This will indicate the natural waistline. Using tailor's chalk mark a line round your waist on the skirt, level with the lower edge. This line is where the waistband will be attached so make sure the skirt is hanging correctly. Any surplus fabric at the waist should extend above the interfacing. Look at the length of the skirt; turn up and pin a short length of front hem at a suitable level.
Remove interfacing. Take off skirt.
Mark any alterations to the side seams. Remove all pins. Make a chalk mark at the hem and remove the pins.
Re-tack any alterations including back seam if necessary, and try on again.
Stitch and finish back seam.
Check the opening left for the zip by placing your zip beside the seam with the slider 5mm ($\frac{1}{4}$in) below the chalked waist line (a little more on thick fabrics). Make a chalk mark at the zip base point on the wrong side if the original mark made after cutting out is now incorrect.
Remove the second row of side seam tacking. The zip edge tacking may be left in.
On the wrong side rule a seam line using tailor's chalk and a ruler. Stitch, press open and neaten both side seams, stopping and fastening off the left seam at the zip mark.

5 Zip
The following instructions are for the overlapping method of inserting a conventional nylon or metal zip, but a concealed zip can equally well be used. See the instructions for the pleated skirt on page 40.
A wide fold of fabric on the front edge of the garment ensures that the teeth of the zip remain covered in wear.
On light weight fabrics it helps to achieve a good result if a narrow strip of light iron-on interfacing is attached to the wrong side of the garment front.
Remove the tacking from the fold first.
Fold under the seam allowance on the garment front, tack and press. This forms the wide fold.
Place the zip right side down to right side of garment back. Line up the zip so that the teeth run on the fitting line and the slider is 5mm ($\frac{1}{4}$in) below the skirt fitting line at the top. Tack beside the zip teeth.
Attach zip foot to the machine and stitch close to the teeth working from the bottom of the tape up to the waist edge.
Remove tackings and press stitching with toe of iron.

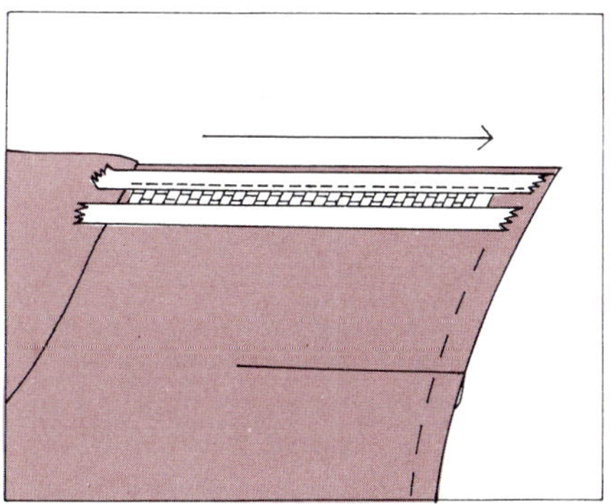

Fold zip over so that it is right side up, smooth the fabric back from the teeth and tack beside the teeth. Press with toe of iron.

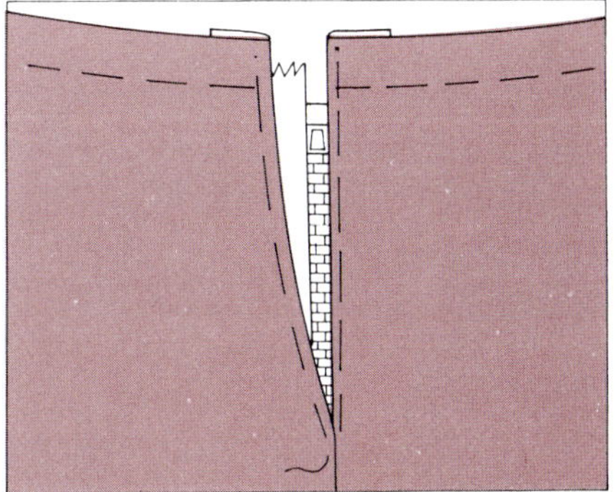

Bring front edge of opening over to cover the teeth and you will see that the advantage of placing the teeth side of the zip carefully was to position it well under the wider fold of fabric.
Holding the edge in place over the zip, start at the bottom and oversew the fold to the garment. Use tacking thread and make sure the fabric is smooth at the base of the zip.
Insert a row of tacking beside the teeth through the front of the garment and zip tape on wide edge. Mark an accurate stitching line beside the teeth (but not too close or a ridge will result) using a chalk pencil or sharp tailor's chalk. A row of dots is the easiest mark to make. Stitch the zip from base to waistline to avoid bulge at the bottom.
Use hand prick stitch or attach the zip foot and machine. Fasten off neatly at the base. It is best not to stitch across the zip below the teeth as it causes a bulge and makes the zip more obvious.
Remove all tackings. To press, place a towel over the pressing surface and then use the toe of the iron to press the line of stitching only.

6 Lining
Buy the best quality lining fabric you can afford. Cheap fabric is often a false economy as it will be less durable and may need replacing before the skirt wears out.
The lining will be finished at a level 3cm ($1\frac{1}{4}$in) shorter than the skirt and it can have a narrow hem. You could economise by cutting the lining pieces 5cm (2in) shorter if you wish.
Cut out pattern pieces you pinned to the lining fabric earlier (11, 12, 13), adding about 3mm ($\frac{1}{8}$in) to all edges except the centre front fold.
This extra amount is needed for movement as lining fabric has little or no give. With thick fabrics you will find the extra amount is automatically added simply because you cannot get the scissors very close to the fabric edge.
Mark darts and zip point. If fitting adjustments were made on the skirt also chalk these on the lining. Stitch darts and seams. Narrow finish or open seams may be used on the lining.
Remember to leave the zip opening on the right seam and make it 1cm ($\frac{3}{8}$in) longer than on the skirt.
After inserting the zip in the skirt, slip the lining inside the skirt with wrong sides facing. Match up seams, centre fronts, darts and centre back and baste the two together round the waist.
From the outside, baste from waist to hem down each seam for half the length of the skirt.
On the inside snip the lining turnings just below the end stop of the zip. Tack turnings to zip tape. Hem each side.

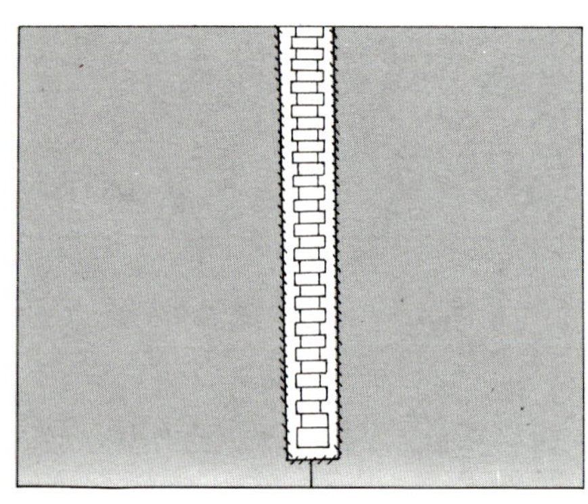

Tack the skirt hem where marked, with one row near the fold and the second 2cm (¼in) above to hold the edge. Turn up and tack the lining hem so that it is 3cm (1¾in) shorter. If you have a hem gauge you can omit this stage.

7 Hanging loops
Cut a strip of narrow petersham ribbon or straight seam binding 25cm (10in) long. Cut the strip in two and fold each piece in half and press. Place on the inside of the skirt, one at the side seam and one on the front beside the zip. Baste in place.

8 Waistband
Pass waistband interfacing round your waist so that it fits. Remove and cut it to length plus an overlap of 5cm (2in). Attach interfacing to fabric by pressing if it is an iron-on banding, or by basting. The waistband pattern piece has been provided in the correct width for perforated iron-on waist-banding. Make sure the interfacing lies on the straight grain of the fabric. Cut out round the interfacing, adding a seam allowance all round. On heavy fabric work a row of machining along the central perforations of the iron-on waistbanding. With non-adhesive types, machine or herringbone along each edge.
Place band to skirt, right sides together and raw edges together, but matching the edge of the interfacing to the chalked waistline mark. Allow the extension on the band to extend above the top of the zip on the skirt back. Insert pins, vertically, at zip edges, seams and darts.
Tack the waistband to the skirt, easing in any apparent fullness on the skirt. Remove pins. Try on and adjust if necessary.
Machine the band to the waist stitching through the waistband skirt and lining, using the edge of the waistband interfacing as a guide.
(See next diagram.)
Remove tackings. Press the seam allowances open all round the waist then press both up into the band. Press from inside skirt then turn it over and press from the right side. Trim the

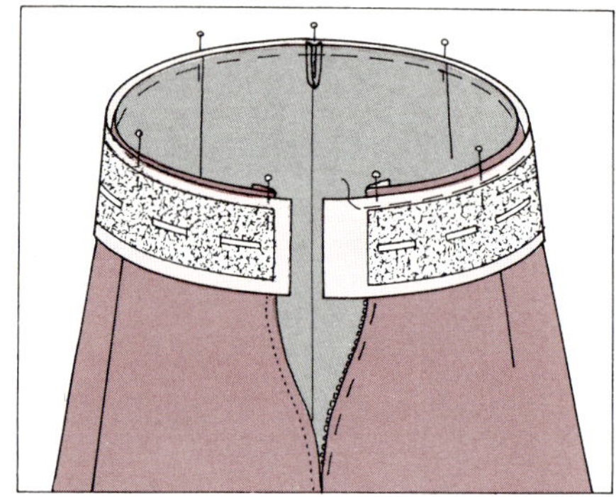

waistband edge down to 3mm (⅛in) and the skirt edge to 5mm (¼in).
Trim the raw edge of the waistband, taking off 5mm (¼in) and neaten the edge. Baste down the centre of the band with the neatened edge extending on to the lining.
At the top of the zip trim down the raw edges of band a little. Turn in so that the folds meet: slip stitch together. On the extension snip the neatened edge and turn it under. Turn under outer edge of band to meet it, tack together and slip stitch. Finish by top stitching all round or working prick stitch from the right side, in the waistband join.

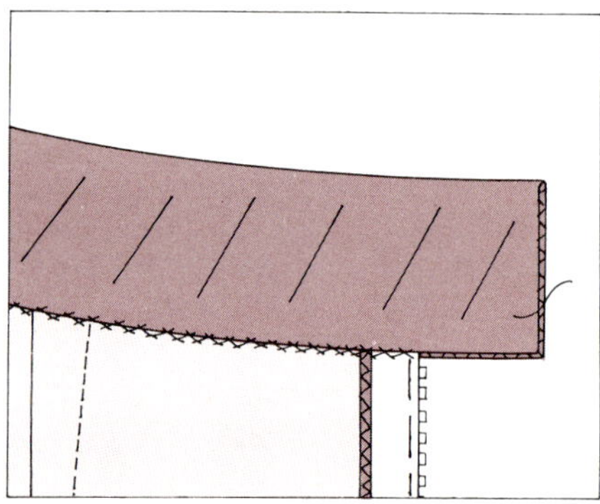

Remove all tackings. Attaching the waistband has automatically enclosed the raw edges of the hanging loops. Attach waist fastening.

9 Large hook and bar
Hooks Try on the garment. Fasten the waistband by pinning and make a chalk mark where the waistband ends. Take off skirt and place the hook almost at the end of the outer piece of band and attach the head by working six stitches taken deeply into the band and under the head of the hook.

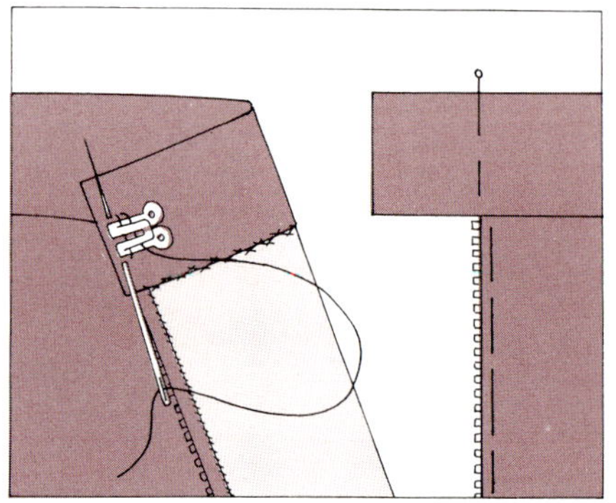

Take the needle through the fabric and come up beside the loop. Work close buttonhole stitch round each part of the loop.
Always use a bar rather than an eye. Fasten the hook into the bar and place the band in position level with the chalk mark. Carefully insert one pin to hold the bar in position, undo the hook and attach the bar with buttonhole stitch.
Alternatively, a trouser clip, Velcro or a button and buttonhole could be used.

10 Hem
Mark the point where the hem is to be folded up with pins or chalk. Remove all tacking. Turn up the hem accurately as follows: arrange the skirt in front of you, right side out and hem towards you. Fold back the upper layer and turn up the hem with the marking on the fold. Keep the skirt flat to avoid stretching. Tack a short section of hem, inserting the stitches no more than 5mm (¼in) above the fold. Fasten off the tacking. Revolve the skirt and repeat on the opposite side of the hem – preferably dealing with it logically, e.g. centre front section followed by centre back. At this stage ignore the slight surplus fabric in the hem edge and concentrate on tacking a smooth fold with no angles. This is the part of the skirt that will always be seen.

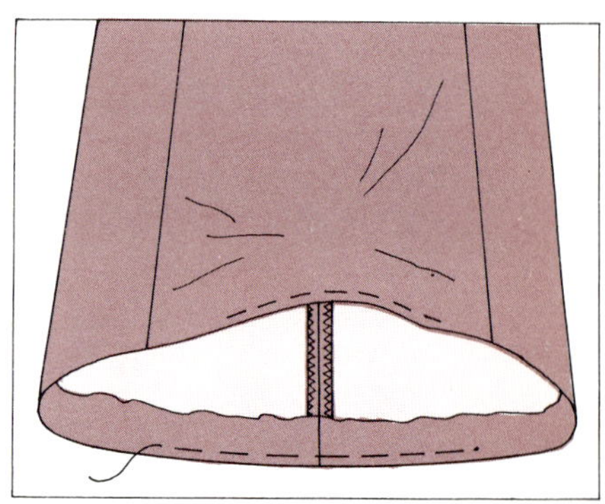

Revolve the skirt twice more and complete the tacking. After fitting trim away the surplus seam edges that fall within the hem depth to reduce bulk. Turn skirt right side out. Arrange hemline on sleeve board and press. Press the fold only, taking care not to stretch the edge. Allow each part to cool before moving.
If you have an adjustable marker, set it to a suitable depth – ideally between 3 and 6cm (1¼–2½in). Work all round to mark the depth on the hem surplus. Work a row of straight machine stitching on this chalk line. This acts as a guide, prevents fraying and reduces any tendency to stretch, especially in jersey fabrics. Trim the surplus fabric off 2mm (1/16 in) from the stitching. Stitch again, this time

working zig-zag or other wide stitch right over the edge and the straight stitching, or overcast by hand.

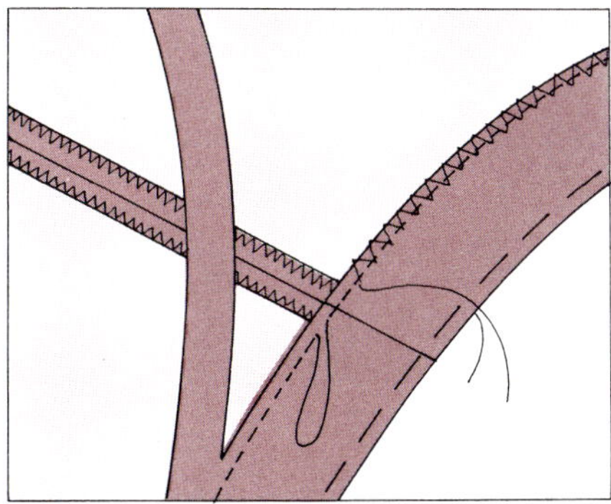

Open out the hem itself and press the stitching to flatten it, but take great care not to stretch the edge.
Arrange skirt on table right side up as before, folding back the upper layer. Tack the hem to the garment stitching just below the neatened edge and using fairly small stitches. Any surplus that was apparent earlier should now be under control.

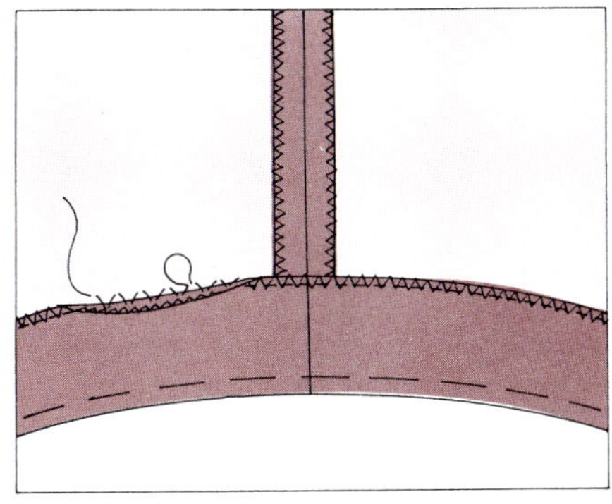

Finish the hem by working catch stitch. Lift up the neatened edge and work stitches between the edge and the skirt. Do not pull the thread tight. Pick up only one thread of the skirt fabric and make stitches no longer than 5mm ($\frac{1}{4}$in). On jersey or loose fabrics leave a short loop of excess thread every 10cm (4in) that can be taken up in the stretch of the fabric.
Check the position of the lining hem by laying out the skirt inside out. Trim surplus lining. Either turn up a wide hem and slip-hem by hand or make the hem narrow and finish with a row of straight, zig-zag or decorative machining. Work bartacks 2cm ($\frac{3}{4}$in) long between lining and skirt at all seams.
To finish: press the skirt from the right side, pressing lightly over the hem to avoid marking it. Run a cooler iron over the lining.
Hang up the skirt to cool.

PLEATED SKIRT

A softly styled skirt with an inverted unpressed pleat at the centre front and two tucks each side. The back is the same as for the panelled skirt. The skirt has one pocket in the right side seam, a zip in the left seam, and optional top stitching on the centre pleat and band.

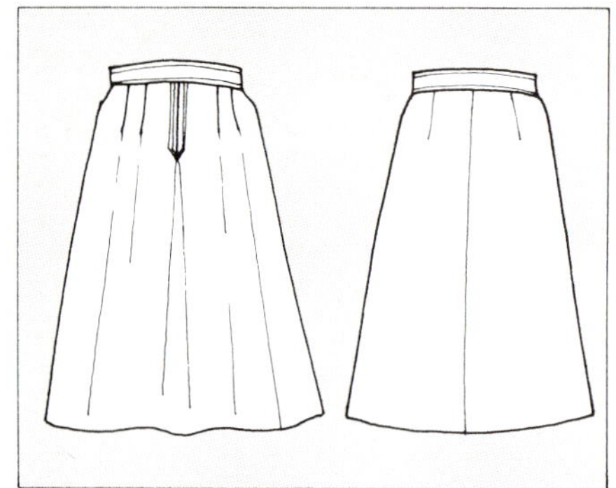

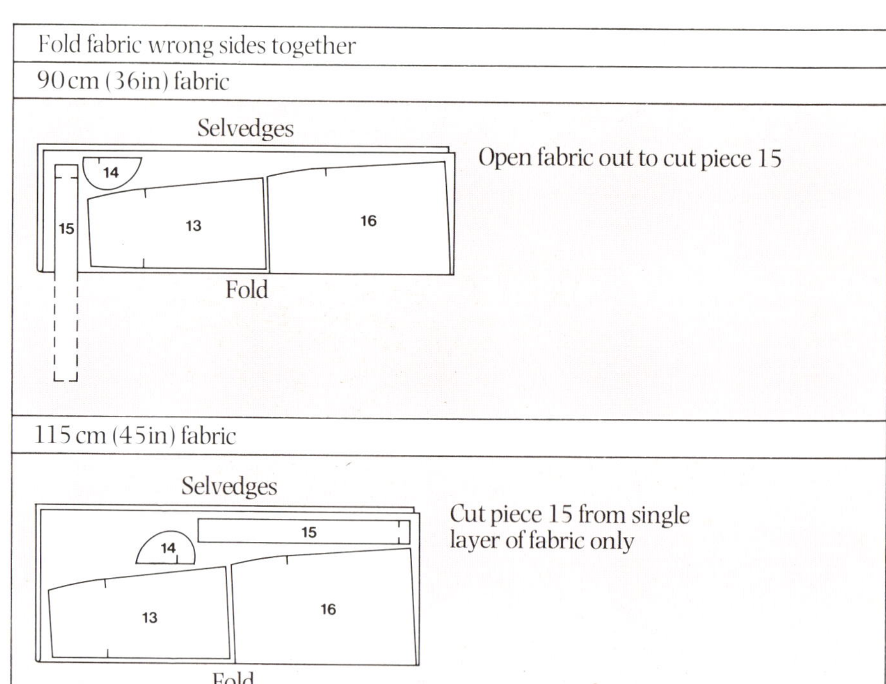

FABRIC

This gently shaped skirt will suit most figures and it can be made in any light or medium fabric. We made it in black wool crêpe to team with the short jacket (see page 18), and in red moygashel with small white spots (see front cover). You could also use polyester cotton, madras, poplin or viscose.

Quantities

Width	*Size*	*Quantity*
90cm (36in)	10	1.60m
	12	1.60m
	14	1.60m
	16	1.65m
	18	1.65m
115cm (45in)	10	1.45m
	12	1.45m
	14	1.45m
	16	1.50m
	18	1.50m

The skirt may be lined Buy the same quantity of lining as fabric.
Interfacing is needed for pocket and stiffening for waistband.
Finished length (not including waistband: 64.5cm (25¼in).

HABERDASHERY

2 reels thread
or 3 if double stitching

20cm (8in) concealed zip

Small piece of light, iron-on interfacing for pocket

Waist length of stiffening for waistband

Fastening as for panelled skirt (page 29)

PATTERN PIECES

13, 14, 15 and 16.
Check and adjust the lengths as necessary.

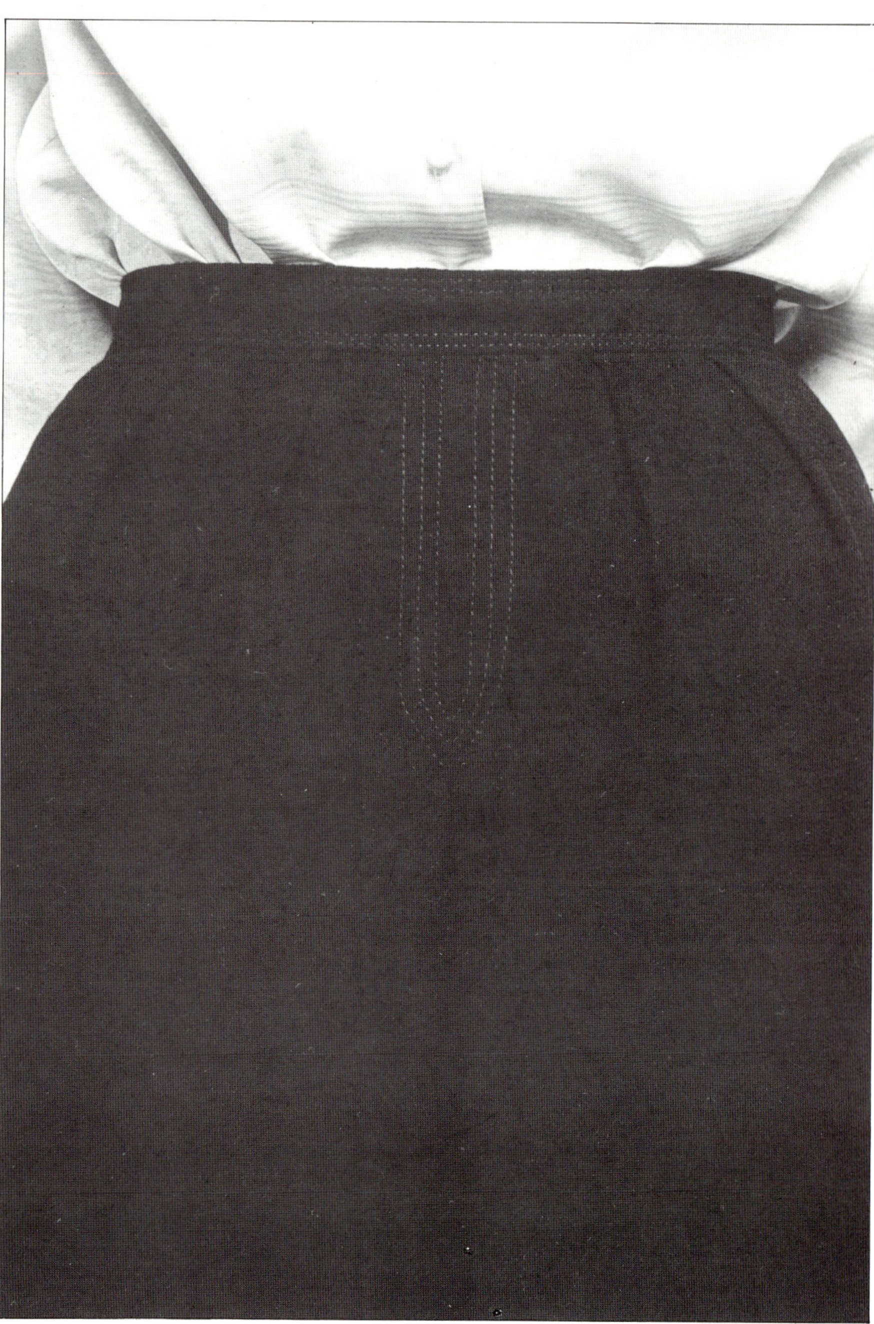

Frilled blouse (page 52) in navy silk with small white spots, worn with a matching pleated skirt (page 33).

Camisole (page 68) and matching pleated skirt (page 33) in yellow, flowered silk.

The camisole and skirt worn with a coat-length version of the basic jacket in matching chiffon.

Evening jacket (page 21) in brocade; camisole (page 68) in cream silk; trousers (page 59) in black jersey. Man's robe (page 23) in black paisley façonné.

CUTTING OUT

Cut out 14, pocket, in iron-on interfacing. Cut out 13 and 16 in fabric following layout diagram. Open out remaining fabric and cut one pocket piece. Press the interfacing to the wrong side of the spare fabric and cut out. Leave the waistband until it is needed.

Marking
Mark the darts, tucks, pleat, pocket and zip positions. Mark balance mark on pocket pieces.

MAKING UP

1 Darts
Follow instructions for panelled skirt (page 29).

2 Centre back seam
Follow instructions for panelled skirt.

3 Pleat
Fold skirt front wrong sides together with centre front marking at the edge. Insert a pin across the fold. Tack on the pleat mark to a depth of 10cm (4in). Try on and adjust length if necessary. If you wish to stitch the pleat, machine on the tacking and fasten off. On some figures it will be better to omit the stitching and let the pleat hang loose but leave it tacked until the skirt is finished.
With wrong side up, place skirt on pressing surface. Line up the centre mark over the join beneath, flatten with your fingers and press. Turn skirt over and press the right side. Baste across the pleat through all layers 5cm (2in) down from waist edge then machine across but only 1cm ($\frac{3}{8}$in) below waist edge. This pressing and stitching should be carried out even if the pleat is not to be stitched at the centre front.

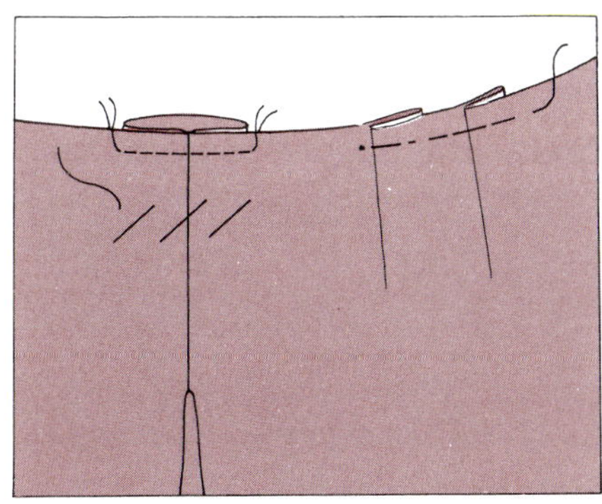

If you wish to add decorative top stitching on each side of the join do it now. The close-up photograph on the left shows the centre front with three rows of top stitching.

Double thread top stitching
This is worked with two reels of thread on the top of the machine, both threaded in the usual way through the machine and through the eye of the needle. It is not necessary to use a larger machine needle. If you have only one thread spindle on your machine wind two spools and place them one on top of the other. Thread each separately through the machine and through the needle. Insert the spool underneath in the usual way. Test the stitching on a folded scrap of fabric. If it wrinkles use a smaller stitch. If it looks unsuitable use a single thread.
Use the edge of the machine foot as a guide for keeping straight. Work the first row of stitching the width of the foot from the pleat line or fabric edge. Work the second beside it still using the foot as a guide. Always stitch on the right side. If you prefer the stitching on the pleat to be further from the centre, draw a line with tailor's chalk. It is very important that the point of the stitching on the pleat should be accurate so mark this with tailor's chalk before you begin.
Start at the waist to the left of the pleat seam and machine to the angled chalk line. Stop with the needle in the fabric exactly on the line, raise the foot and swivel the skirt. Lower the foot in line with the chalk line. Stitch until you reach the pleat seam counting the number of stitches. Stop with the needle in the fabric, lift the foot, turn, lower the foot and proceed along the other angled chalk line, working the same number of stitches as before. Turn again and stitch up to the waist. The second row is easier. Simply keep the edge of the foot level with the first row of stitching, turning each time with the needle in the fabric. A third row may be added.
Cut off all ends of thread. Press the stitching on the wrong side and then on the right side.

4 Tucks
With fabric right side up, fold so that marked tuck lines meet. The tucks face towards the centre so the bulk of the fabric lies towards the side of the garment. Tack near the fold for a distance of 5cm (2in) into the garment. Tack down the tucks, and baste across the top of them 1cm ($\frac{3}{8}$in) from the waist edge.
When you fit the skirt the waist size may need adjusting. If so, these tucks can be reduced or made deeper.

5 Pocket and side seams
Place fabric pocket piece right side down to right side of back skirt, at the right seam. Match the balance marks on the pocket and skirt. Tack and machine from balance mark to top of pocket but stopping 1.5cm ($\frac{5}{8}$in) from the edge and taking only 5mm ($\frac{1}{4}$in) turning on the seam. Remove tacking.

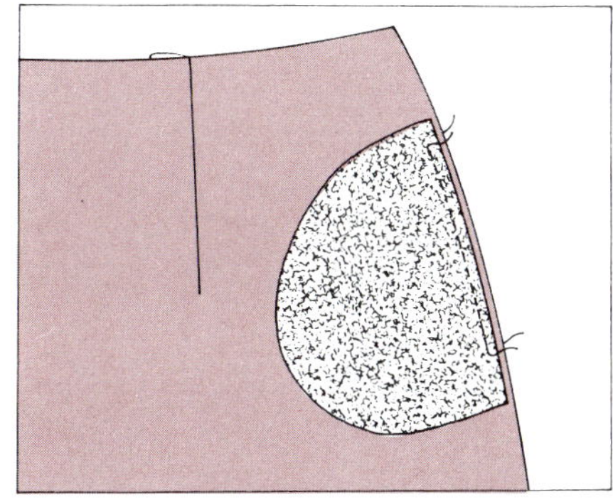

Place front skirt to back, right sides together, matching side edges. Tack and machine side seam starting level with the top of the pocket and stitching to the waist. Then machine from the base of the pocket, stitching to the hem.

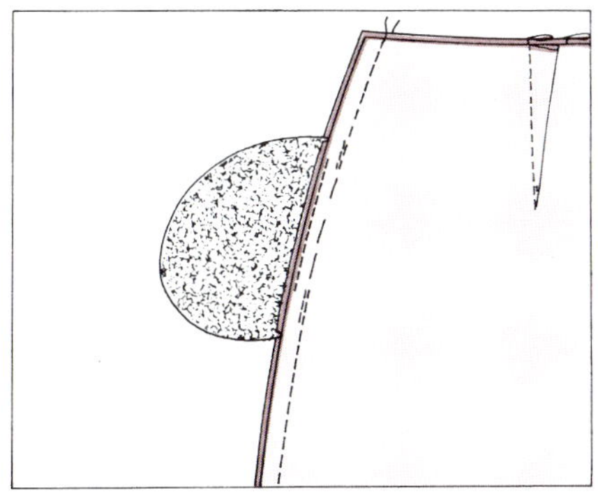

Place interfaced pocket piece to edge of front skirt seam right sides together. Make sure the piece is exactly level with the other pocket section. Machine, taking 5mm ($\frac{1}{4}$in) turning. Press open both pocket seams.

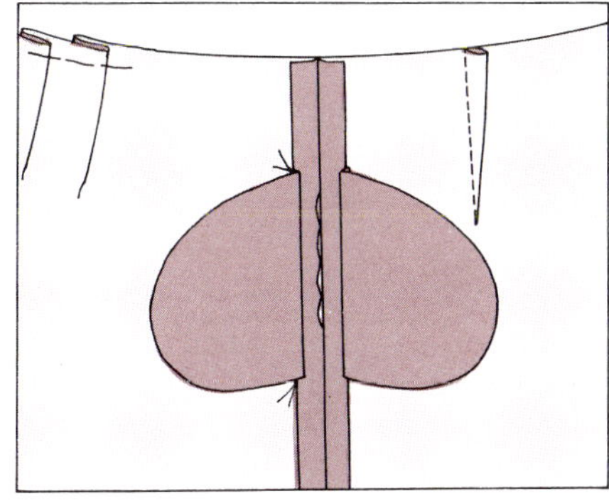

Press both pocket pieces towards front of skirt but keeping the skirt seam open, with skirt right side up, and press to make sure the seam and the pocket opening lie flat in one continuous neat line. The pocket should be unobtrusive. To prevent it moving tack through all layers close to the pocket opening from the right side.

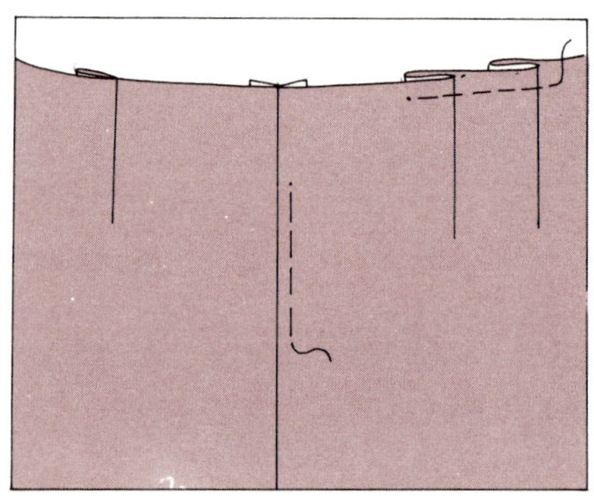

On the wrong side baste the pocket pieces together. Mark a stitching line round the outside and machine on it. At the top fasten off on the end of the pocket stitching. At the base turn the corner and stitch up until you reach the other end of the pocket stitching, holding the pocket so that it extends beyond the skirt.

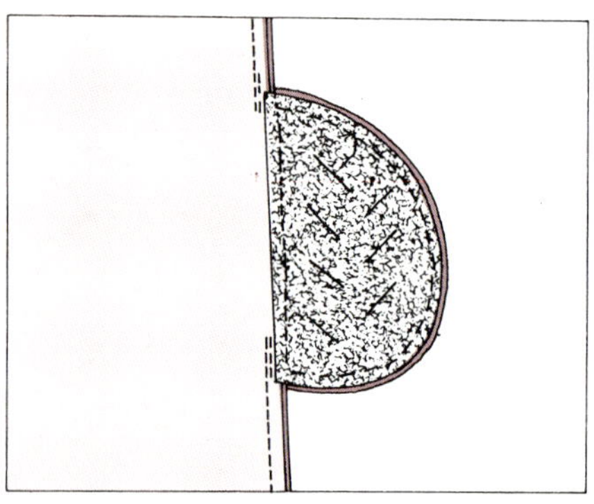

Note To achieve a flat effect on the right side of the skirt, it is best not to try to join up the ends of the rows of machining. Stitch as far as you reasonably can and fill any gaps with hemming, back stitch or slip stitch. Forcing two rows of inside machining to meet will result in a bulge, wrinkle or wobbly seam.
Trim the raw edges of pocket to 3 mm ($\frac{1}{8}$ in) and neaten them. Where completed pocket crosses the open side seam, work herringbone stitch to hold it flat and prevent the pocket from moving in wear. Finally neaten all remaining raw edges of the skirt seam, stitching over both edges where the pocket is situated.

6 Zip

Note These instructions are for inserting a concealed zip, but the zip method described for the panelled skirt (page 31) could be used.
Stitch the garment seam. The gap left in the seam should be 1 cm ($\frac{3}{8}$ in) shorter than the length of the zip teeth. Using a larger size stitch, machine from the seam end to the top of the zip position.
Press the seam open. Neaten both edges for the length of garment.
With fabric wrong side up, place zip right side down on the seam. Make

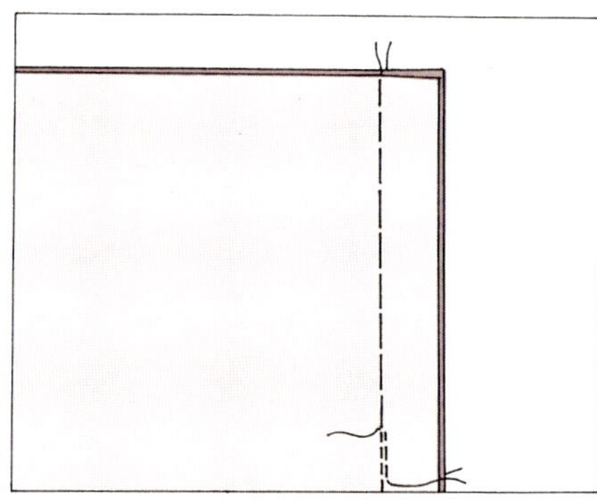

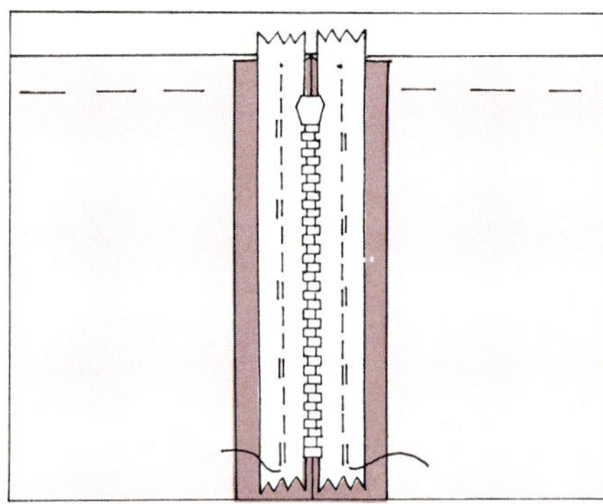

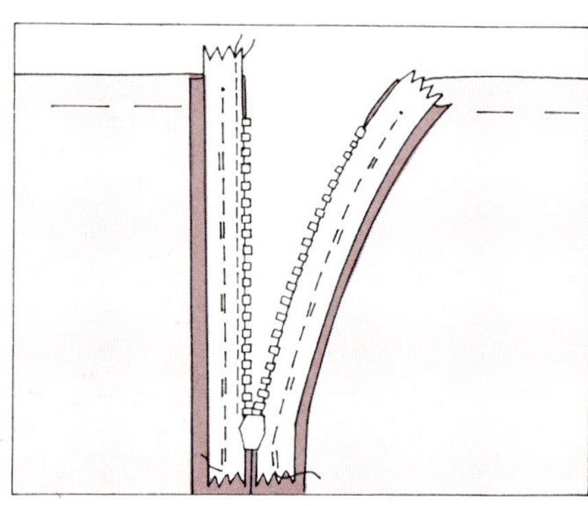

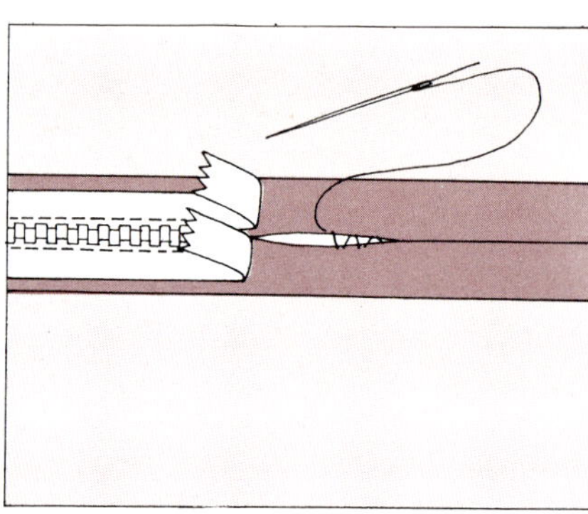

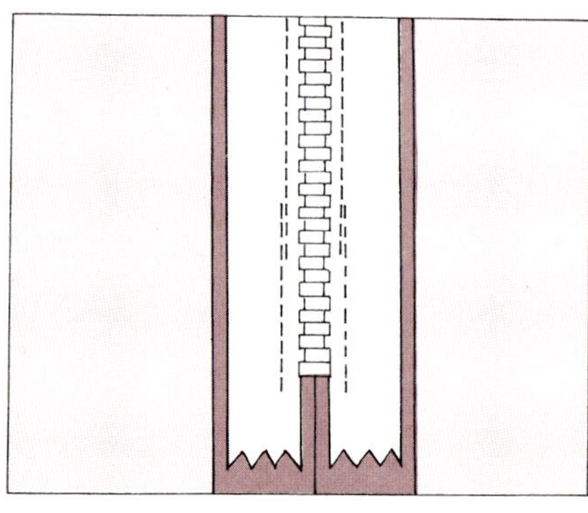

sure the zip slider is a little below the fitting line of the garment. Tack from top to bottom on each side through the zip tape and the seam allowance. Prevent the needle from penetrating the garment by sliding your fingers under the seam allowance. Take a back stitch every third stitch as this zip has a tendency to slide out of place. Make sure the centre of the teeth lies exactly over the seam line. Attach zip foot to machine.
Remove the large machining open the zip and stitch the tape to the turnings. To do this, roll the teeth over as flat as possible so that the stitching can be placed as close to the teeth as possible. Use a medium length machine stitch and sew with the zip teeth uppermost. Stitch to the slider. Stitch the other side in the same way. Remove the tacking stitches. If possible machine in the same direction each side.
Close the zip. Turn the garment wrong side up, lift the lower end of the zip and slip stitch by hand to close the gap from below the zip, stitching to the top of the seam stitching. Pick up a small amount of fabric from each fold of fabric alternately. Do not pull the thread tight. Fasten off. Re-tack the bottom part of the zip tape to the seam allowances and stitch as close as possible to the teeth. Machine or back stitch by hand.
If the skirt is to be lined place pattern pieces 13 and 16 on lining but omit the pleat from the skirt front. Do this by moving the pattern over so that it extends beyond the fold of fabric.

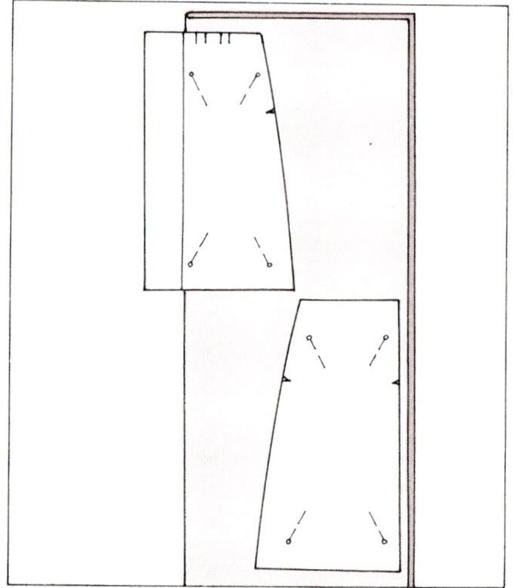

Make up the lining and insert hanging loops as for panelled skirt (page 31).

7 Waistband

Fit Put on the skirt and fasten the zip. Adjust the front tucks if necessary. Put the waistband interfacing round your waist over the skirt and pin. Mark a chalk line on the skirt level with the lower edge. Mark the exact size of your waist on the interfacing. Take off the skirt.
Attach waistband interfacing to wrong side of waistband.
Place waistband to skirt waist right

sides together. Pin the end level with the top of the zip at the front with 1.5cm ($\frac{5}{8}$in) extending. Pin the other end beside so that the underlap extends. Insert a few more pins round the waist. Check that stitching will fall on the marked waist line, then tack from skirt side through band and skirt. Machine in position, working from waistband side following the interfacing and stitching just off the edge of it.

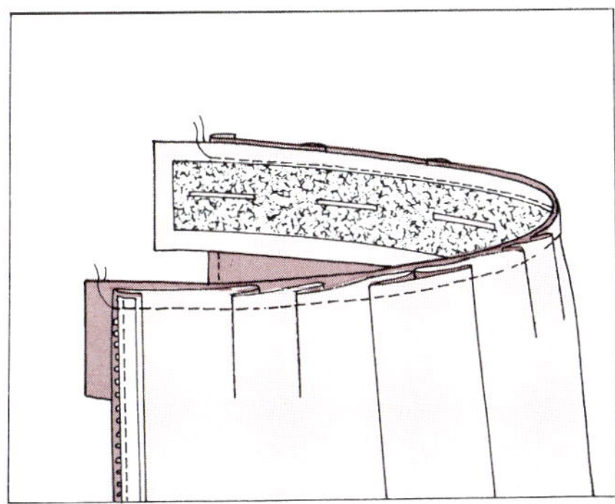

Remove tacking, trim turning a little. Press the join so that the turnings lie up into the band. Tack from right side just above join to hold turnings in place. Turn over the ends of the band and also the lower edge of the extension and hold down with herringbone stitch. Reduce the bulk by trimming the raw edges down to about 5mm ($\frac{1}{4}$in). Press.

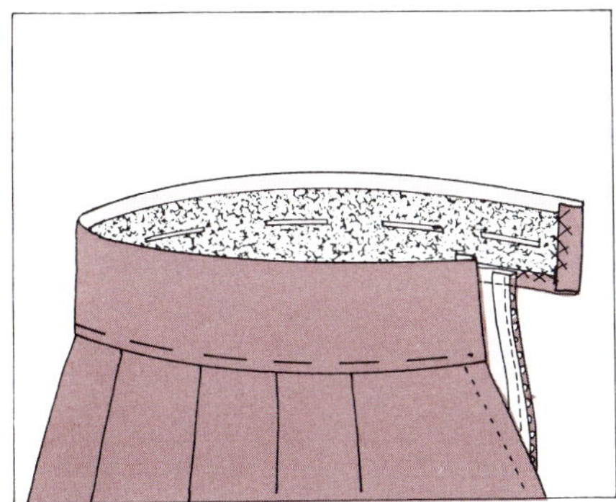

Fold band over to wrong side of skirt, tack and press the fold. Tack the ends together and the extension and slip stitch. Along the remainder of the band trim a little off the edge to reduce bulk then turn under and hem into the machine stitching.

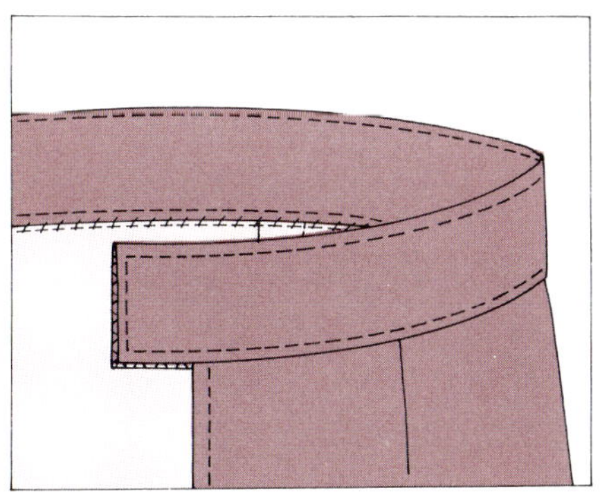

Remove tackings. Press. Top stitch the waistband by working single or double machining all round, working on the right side of the band through all layers of fabric. Press.
Attach fastening.

8 Hem

Follow instructions for panelled skirt (page 32).

BLOUSE

A timeless classic shirt-style blouse with pointed collar and neck band, shoulder tucks to provide shaping and long sleeves gathered into cuffs. We made it in silk crêpe with woven satin spot and top stitched all the edges to give it a formal shirt finish.

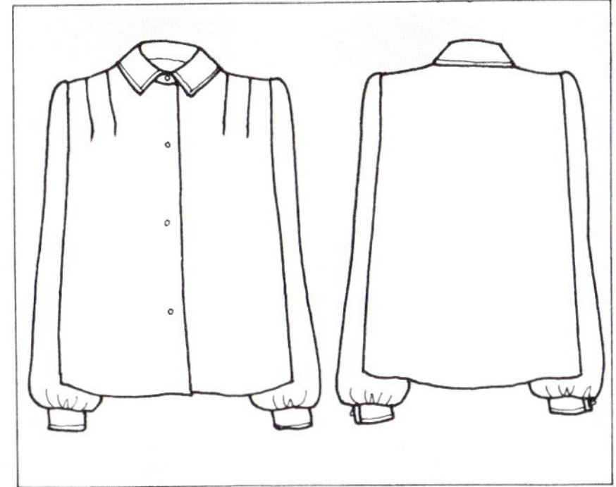

FABRIC

Our choice was silk crêpe, but you could use shirting, lawn, shantung, polyester cotton or viyella.
The cover photograph shows the shirt blouse teamed with the panelled skirt and the basic jacket. It is also shown on page 33.

Quantities

Width	*Size*	*Quantity*
90cm (36in)	10	2.65m
	12	2.65m
	14	2.70m
	16	2.75m
	18	2.75m
115cm (45in)	10	1.85m
	12	1.90m
	14	2.05m
	16	2.10m
	18	2.15m

Interfacing is needed for front edges, collar and neckband. For a very crisp effect, attach interfacing to both pieces of collar and band.
Interface cuffs with cuff interfacing or use light, iron on interfacing over entire cuff.
Finished length, back neck to hem (size 12): 62cm ($24\frac{1}{2}$in).

HABERDASHERY

- 2 reels thread
- Interfacing (see above)
- Cuff interfacing
- 8 small buttons
- Adhesive web for buttonholes
- An adjustable marker helps to space buttons accurately

PATTERN PIECES

17, 18, 19, 20, 21, 23 and 24. Check and adjust length of pieces 16, 18 and 19 if necessary.

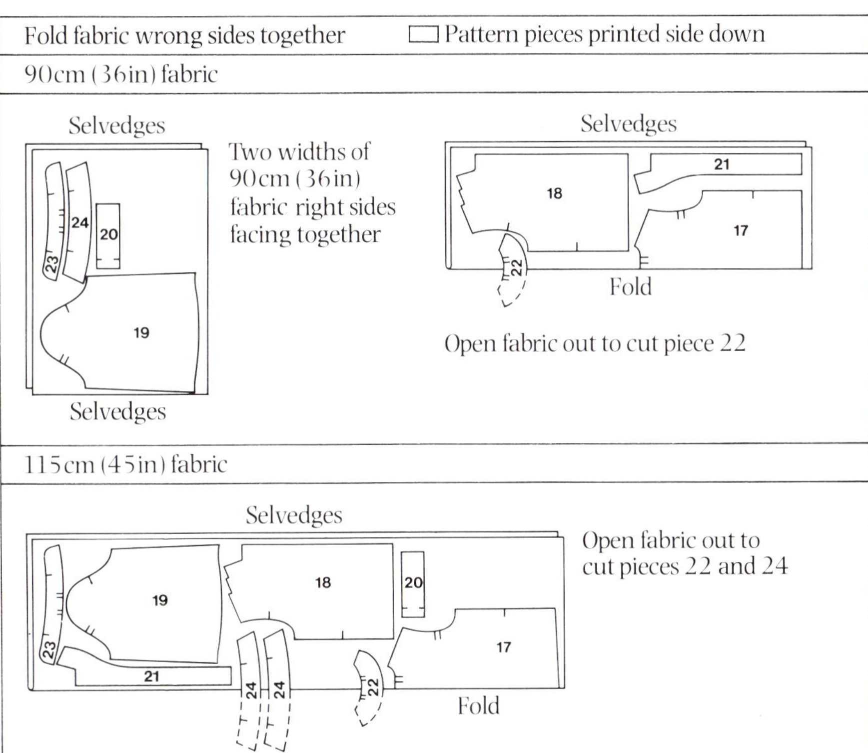

CUTTING OUT

Cut out pieces 21, 23, 24 in interfacing. Cut lengths of cuff band interfacing for cuffs, 20, or cut interfacing the same size as the cuff pattern.
Pin all pieces to fabric. Cut out 17, 18, 19, 21. Leave the smaller pieces until needed. When they are, open out the fabric and press the interfacing for collar, band and cuffs to the wrong side of the fabric taking care that the straight grain is correct. Cut out.

Marking
Mark centre back fold, central point on sleeve head and balance marks on sleeve head and back and front armhole. Mark the shoulder tucks, centre front line and wrist opening position. After cutting out the collar, band and cuffs, mark the cuff extension point, tack the centre back fold of the collar and collar band and mark the balance marks on both.
Mark 1.5cm ($\frac{5}{8}$in) seam allowance round the collar and the band.
Attach the blouse front interfacing to the wrong side of the blouse pieces.

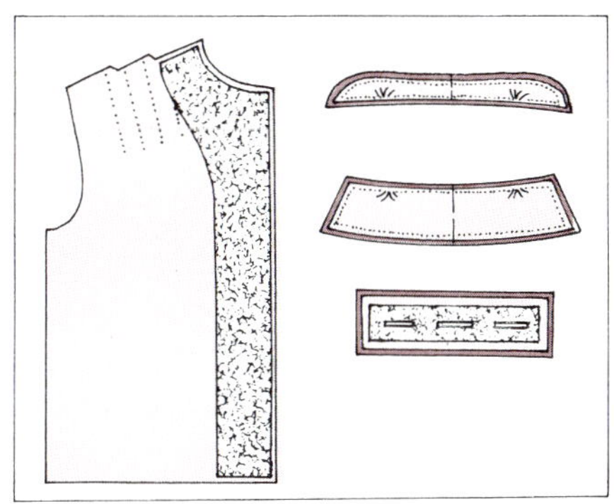

MAKING UP

1 Tucks
Fold blouse front right sides together to pin the shoulder tucks. Match up the markings and tack from shoulder to end of tuck. Machine and fasten off the threads. Press tucks to one side. The bulk of the fabric should lie towards the neck.

2 Shoulder and side seams
Place blouse fronts to blouse back right sides together and with shoulder edges and side edges together. Tack the seams, taking 1.5cm ($\frac{5}{8}$in) seam allowance.
Fit Put on the blouse, and overlap the front edges so that centre lines meet, and pin. If the back of the blouse droops lift the back at the shoulder. If the shoulders are too long, put in a pin as a guide for tacking in the sleeves. Check the width of the blouse at underarm and at hip level. Pin out any excess, or if the seams need letting out, snip the tacking to release them. If you have a narrow back take out the excess width on the back only at the side seams. If you have a rounded back and it causes the back neck to gape, two small darts could be put in the neckline. If you do this remember to shorten the collar and band to correspond, before cutting them out.
Machine the seams, remove tackings and press open. Trim and neaten the raw edges with a zig-zag stitch or overcasting. If the fabric is fine, transparent or frays badly make French seams instead (see page 49).

3 Collar and facing

Neaten the outer edge of the facing pieces. Place facings to blouse fronts right sides together. Tack and machine from neckline to hem taking 1.5 cm ($\frac{5}{8}$ in) seam allowance. Press the joins open, trim the facing edge to 3 mm ($\frac{1}{8}$ in) and the blouse edge to 5 mm ($\frac{1}{4}$ in). Roll the facing to the wrong side, working the join to the edge and then to a position slightly to the inside and tack the edge. Press. Place blouse fronts right side up and baste through blouse and facing.

Put collar pieces together right sides facing, tack and machine on the seam line round outer edge.
At collar points change to a smaller machine stitch for 2 cm ($\frac{3}{4}$ in) on each side. At the point stop, and work one stitch across the corner. This makes the point easier to turn through.

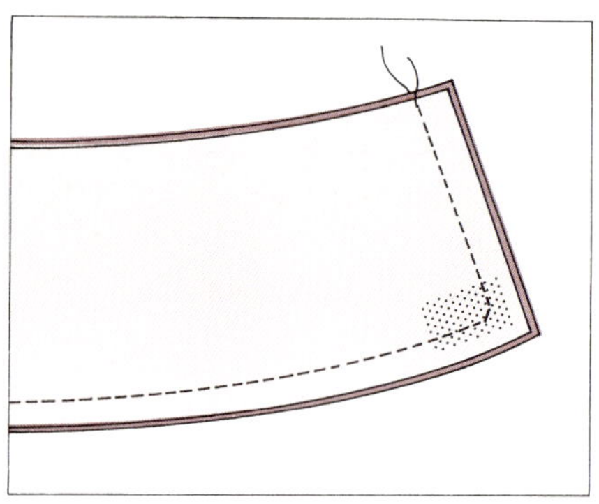

Trim and layer the raw edges and cut off the surplus at the points. If the fabric is soft or frays badly press a very small piece of paper-backed adhesive on top of the stitching at the point. Turn the collar right side out. Roll the edges and work out the points so that the join is right on the outer edge. Tack and press then baste the two raw edges together to hold. Work a row of edge stitching round the outer edge of the collar. Place interfaced band (or the piece which is stiffest) on the table right side up. Place made-up collar on top with its interfaced (stiffer) side down. Match the centre back marks. Tack on seam line. Place other section of collar band right side down on top of collar and tack. Machine round ends of band and across neck to enclose collar. To prevent collar moving, stitch from centre back to end of band, then return and stitch other side, starting at the centre back.

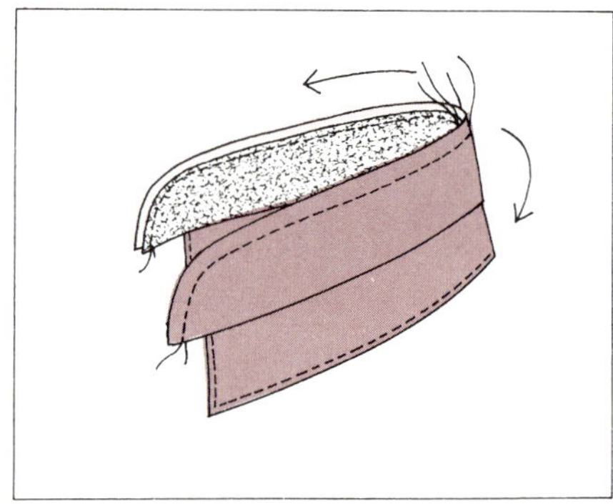

Carefully trim and layer all raw edges and snip at intervals round the band edges. Press the stitching flat then turn bands right side out, pull out collar and press.

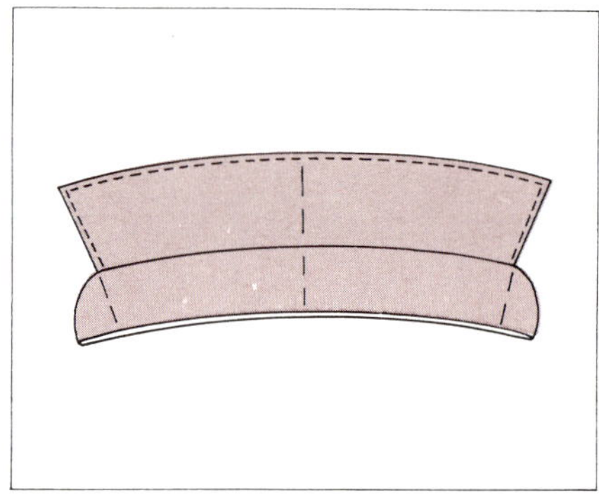

Place interfaced collar band to blouse neck, right sides together.
Match centre back and insert pins vertically. Snip the garment neck edge at intervals so that it meets the band more easily. Tack band to neck, working with garment neck edge towards you. Remove pins. Turn garment round and machine beside the tacking but with band uppermost. The end of the band must meet the faced front edge of the shirt so if this is difficult, fold the turnings inside the band out of the way and machine from centre front edge inwards for about 1 cm ($\frac{3}{8}$ in) to anchor each end before stitching the entire neckline.

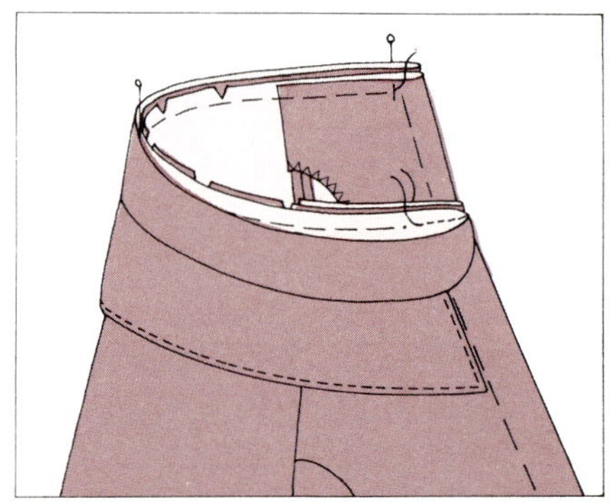

Remove tackings. Trim all neck turnings, preferably to slightly varying widths to avoid a ridge. Extend collar and band upwards so that they stand above the neckline and press the join just made. Baste along the centre of the band through both layers and trim the remaining raw edge down to 1 cm ($\frac{3}{8}$ in) or less to make it easier to handle. Turn under the raw edge so that the fold meets the machine stitching. Insert pins vertically and tack. This edge is inclined to stretch so pin at centre back and centre front, then evenly between. Finish by hemming into every machine stitch. Work a continuous row of machining round the base of the band to match the collar. Remove tacking and press.

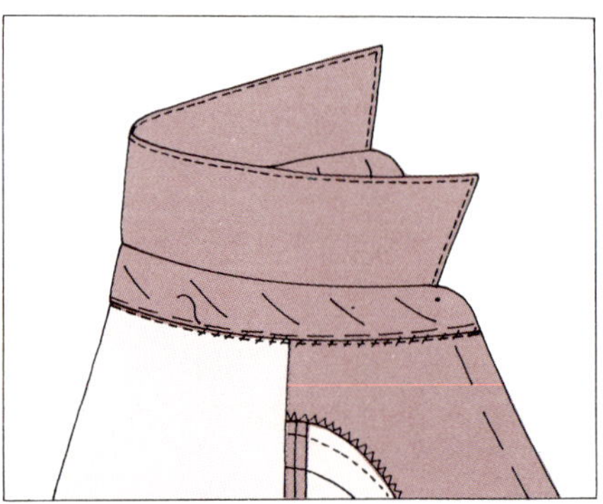

Put on the blouse, match the centre front lines and pin. Pin the neck band. Check the fit of the neck band and insert several pins in the blouse beside the front edge and band to mark the amount of wrap-over. Take off the blouse and put a row of tacking over the pins. Remove pins.

4 Hem

Fold blouse in half at centre back with seams and front edges exactly matched. Cut hemline level, trimming edges if necessary. Even if the blouse is the correct length, turning a narrow hem is easier if the edge is freshly cut. Arrange the blouse on table wrong side up and with facings extended. Undo some of the basting if necessary. Begin at centre back and turn a double fold 5 mm ($\frac{1}{4}$ in) wide on fine fabrics or a little more on thicker ones. Tack with small stitches. Take one back stitch at the seam where the hem will be bulky. Tack a little way past the fold line at the blouse front.

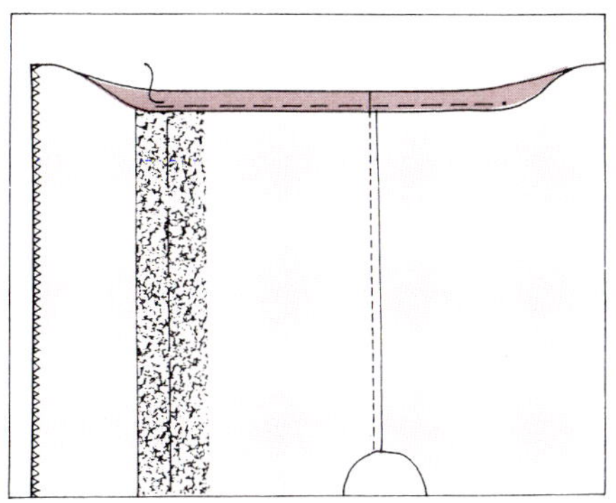

Turn blouse round and tack the other half of the hem in the same way. Press the hem. Check that the two front edges are the same length by folding the facings back and putting the edges together. Machine the hem on the fold. Two rows may be used, one on the bottom edge of the blouse. A small zig-zag or other decorative stitch may be used instead of a straight stitch or it can be slip hemmed by hand. Remove all tackings and press.
With right side up, fold under the facings and tack down the front edge and again near the outer edge.

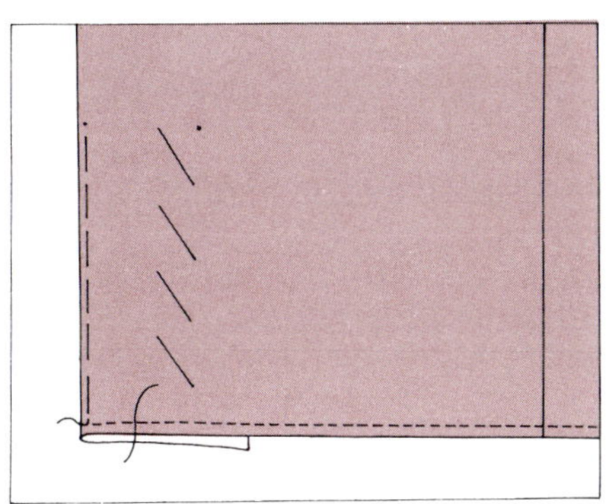

On the wrong side turn under the edge of the facing so that it is a little way inside the blouse hem edge. Tack. Slip stitch along the bottom from the corner to the edge of the facing then hem where the facing crosses the hem. Remove tacking and press.

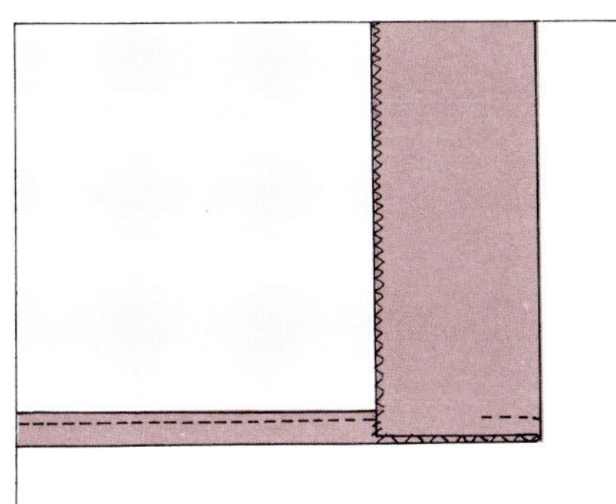

Complete the top stitching starting at one hem corner, stitching up to the neck band, round the curve and neck and down the other front edge.

5 Sleeve opening

The faced slit opening is suitable for all fabrics. Using a small piece of adhesive strip in construction will prevent fraying and it will also help hold the facing flat.
Cut rectangles of fabric 4 cm ($1\frac{1}{2}$ in) wide and 8 cm (3 in) long. Press a narrow strip of adhesive web along the centre but not quite the full length of the fabric. This piece forms the facing of the slit. Trim one end to a curved shape and neaten the curved outer edge.

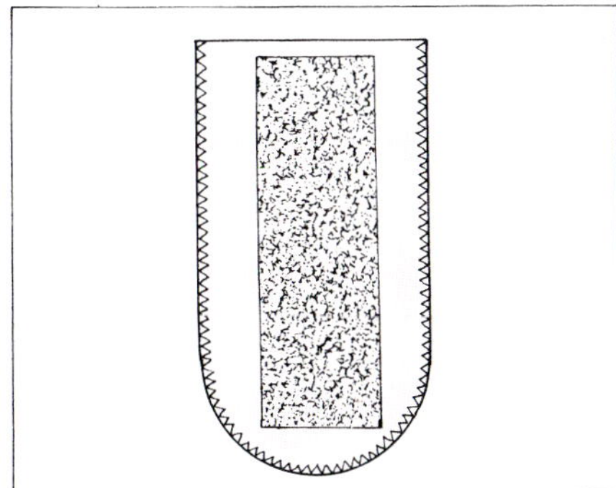

Place facing to sleeve right sides together. Insert 2 pins. Turn sleeve over and insert 3 pins well away from the marked opening. Remove the 2 pins from underneath. Machine beside the marking using the machine foot as a guide. The two rows should be 3–5 mm ($\frac{1}{8}$–$\frac{1}{4}$ in) apart depending on the thickness of the fabric, and a point should be made at the top.

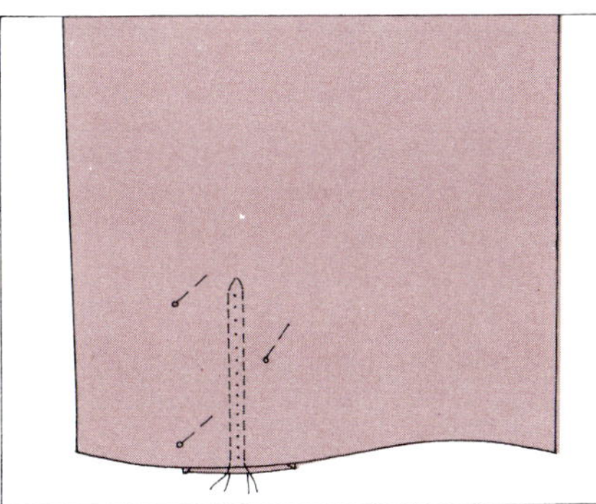

Remove pins. Cut the opening, snipping carefully between the rows of stitching. Roll facing to wrong side and roll and pinch the edges. Press carefully on the edge to make the facing adhere to the sleeve. Trim surplus facing level with sleeve edge.

6 Sleeve seams and cuffs

Fold each sleeve right sides together and tack the seams taking 1.5 cm ($\frac{5}{8}$ in) seam allowance. Make open or French seams (see page 49) to match those on the main part of the blouse.
Insert a gathering thread round the wrist of the sleeve 1.5 cm ($\frac{5}{8}$ in) from the raw edge. Using a large machine stitch, start beside the sleeve opening with sleeve right side up. Reverse for a few stitches to anchor the thread. Finish, leaving a loose end, beside the sleeve opening.
Place cuff to sleeve right sides together, pin at each end matching balance mark; extension should appear at the back of the sleeve. Ensure that you are making a right and a left sleeve and then pull up the gathering thread until the sleeve fits the cuff.

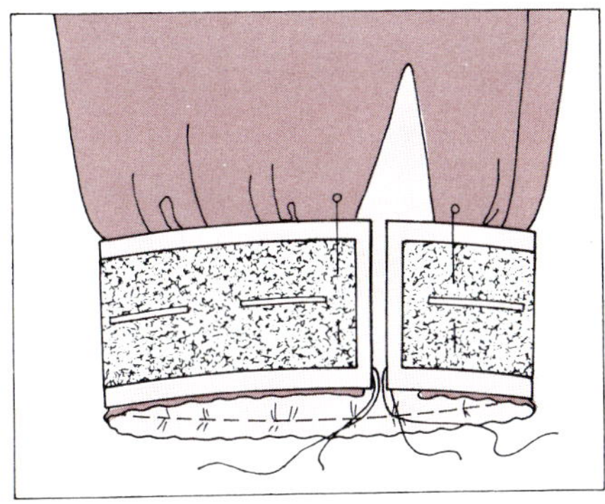

Turn the assembly sleeve side out. Even out the gathering, insert a few pins vertically then tack from cuff side in order to follow edge of interfacing. Remove the pins.
Try on the blouse, then pin the cuff closed and check on the length of the sleeve.

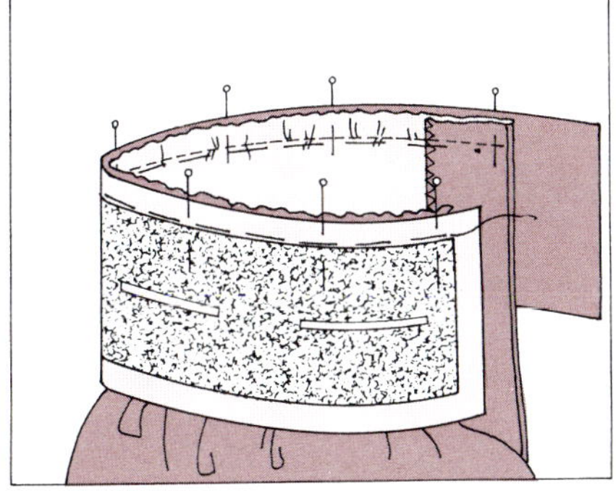

Machine cuff to sleeve from gathered side in order to keep the gathers evenly arranged.
Remove tackings. Remove gathering thread by snipping it at the anchored end and pulling it out.
Trim the turnings to 3 mm ($\frac{1}{8}$ in). Fold cuff in half right sides together and fold on central line of interfacing. Tack. Insert one pin across each end of cuff.
Machine across the cuff ends.

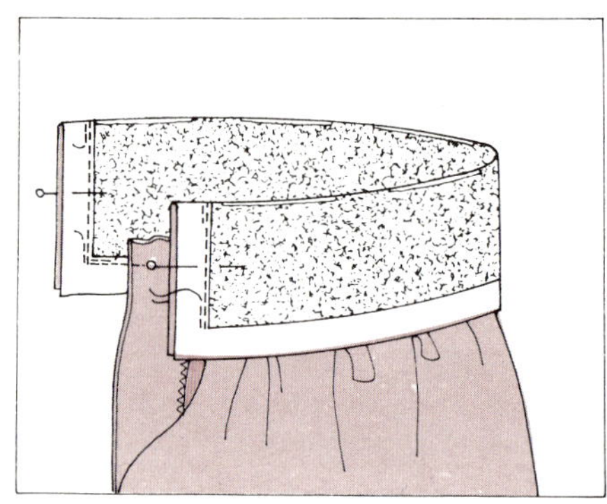

Trim down turnings and cut off corners. Remove tackings and pins. Turn cuffs right side out and work out the corners. Press the cuffs. Turn under the raw edge and tack. The edge should be on the machining. At the lower end of the extension turn under the two edges to meet each other and slip stitch. Press.

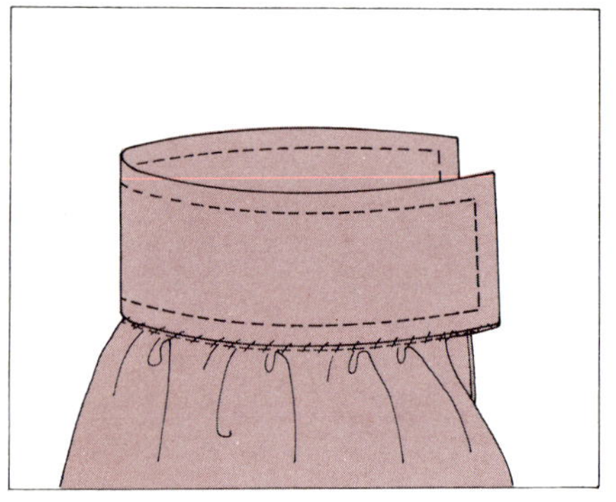

If top stitching is to be done round the cuff, do it now.

7 Buttonholes
Blouse buttons should be fairly small, about 5 mm ($\frac{1}{4}$ in) diameter on fine fabrics and up to 13 mm ($\frac{1}{2}$ in) on thicker fabrics and more casual clothes. The smaller the button the more can be used. Place 6 buttons on the blouse front and space them out. One should be placed in the band collar and the others below. The top button below the collar should be quite near the neckline to prevent it gaping. Insert pins horizontally at approximately the positions you want the buttons. Try on the blouse. Check that one button will be level with your bust line to prevent gaping. Check that you have one above the waist, also possibly one below (except with shirts to be worn outside a skirt) but do not have a button directly under the waistband. Adjust pins if necessary. Take off blouse.
Use an adjustable marker for accuracy. Set it to the correct distance and mark off the spacing on the centre front line using chalk or chalk pencil. Measure diameter of button, add a little for ease and re-set adjustable marker. Mark the length of each buttonhole with chalk or chalk pencil.

The buttonhole in the neck band must be horizontal. Those below may be either horizontal or vertical. The ones in the cuffs must be horizontal.

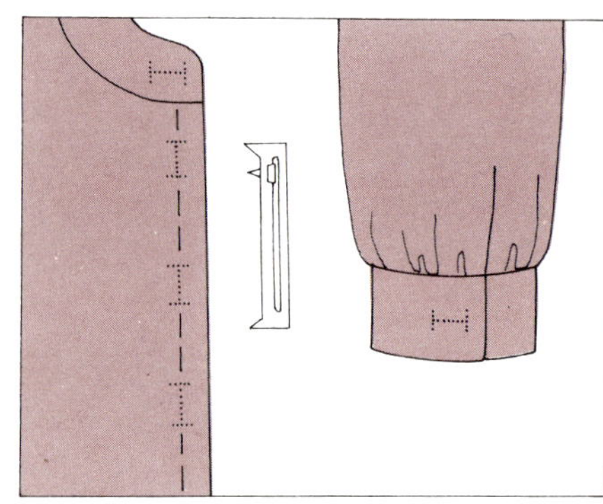

Work buttonholes in front and cuffs.
Machine-made buttonholes
The method of making a buttonhole varies with each machine. Refer to your manual for instructions. The secrets of success lie in careful, accurate preparation.
(a) Tack all round the area to be worked to prevent fabric movement.
(b) Use both interfacing and a strip of adhesive web to reduce fraying.
(c) Use chalk to mark the ends and positions of each buttonhole.
(d) Make a trial buttonhole on spare fabric and test out a button.

8 Setting in sleeves
Follow method given for the basic jacket (page 11).
Press the blouse.

9 Buttons
Before attaching the cuff buttons try on the blouse and pin each cuff to fit comfortably, taking into account wrist watch or bangles. Chalk a line or pin to indicate the extent of the wrap-over. Take off and attach button.
Buttons
It is worth taking time to attach buttons correctly. The most important points are
(a) Use a double thread knotted at the end. Now run the thread through a block of beeswax. The knot can be cut off from the wrong side of the fabric after the first few stitches are secured.
(b) Remember to make a shank which should be just long enough to allow the buttoned area to lie flat.

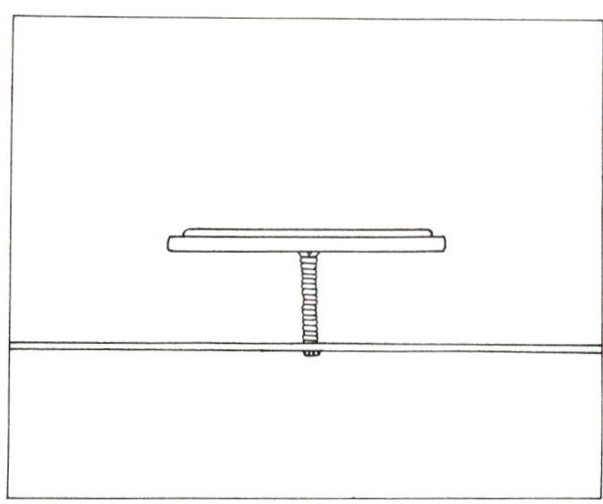

Finish blouse by attaching buttons to front and cuffs.
Run the toe of the iron round each button to remove any wrinkling in the fabric.

On this page we show the four variations that you can make from the basic blouse pattern. All of them have the same basic body construction as the shirt blouse and you will need to refer to the previous pages when making them.
The blouses team well with other garments in the book and the frilled version can be seen in different fabrics on pages 17 and 35.

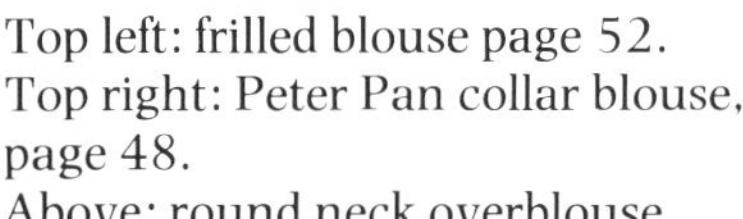
Top left: frilled blouse page 52.
Top right: Peter Pan collar blouse, page 48.

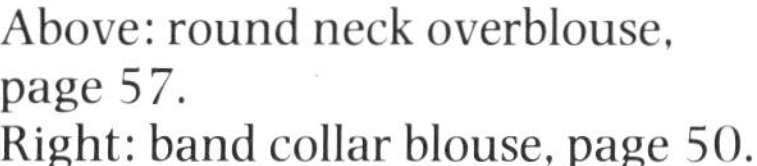
Above: round neck overblouse, page 57.
Right: band collar blouse, page 50.

BLOUSE: PETER PAN COLLAR

This is basically the same as the shirt with the same shoulder tucks for shaping and long sleeves with cuffs. There is no collar band, the Peter Pan-style collar is attached directly to the neck, giving a softer, less formal look. We made it in white polyester and show it here teamed with the pleated skirt (page 33).

FABRIC

Use soft fabrics, plain or printed, such as lawn, batiste, crêpe de chine, synthetic crêpe, georgette, silk or synthetic satin, faillé, viyella, voile, pongée, moss crêpe.

Quantities
As for basic blouse (page 43).
Interfacing is needed for front edges and collar. Use the light sew-in interfacing for fine fabrics and iron-on for heavier fabrics.
Interface cuff with cuff interfacing or with iron-on over the entire cuff.

HABERDASHERY

As for basic blouse (page 43), plus 1 small press stud.

PATTERN PIECES

17, 18, 19, 20, 21 and 25.

CUTTING OUT

Place pieces 25 and 21 on the interfacing and cut out. Pin pattern pieces 21 to 18, overlapping the edge by 1.5cm ($\frac{5}{8}$in).
This can now be placed on the fabric and cut out as one piece to eliminate the join on the front edge. This is an advantage with soft or transparent fabrics.

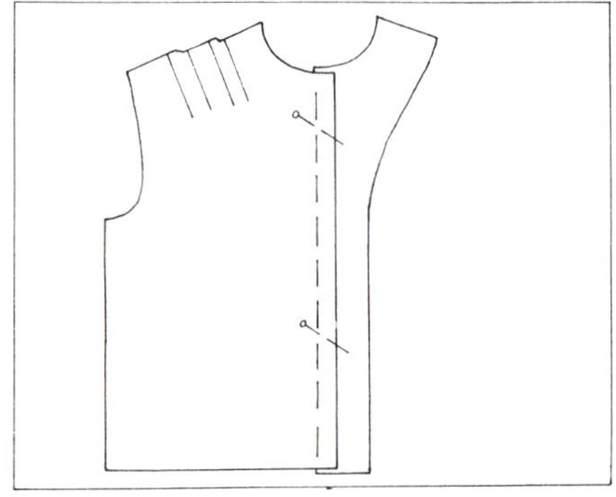

Cut out this piece and also 17 and 19. Leave 20 and 25 until required.

Marking
Mark tucks, centre front line, sleeve head points, sleeve opening, centre back.

MAKING UP

Attach the interfacing to the wrong side of each blouse front, the edge of the interfacing will extend into the facing area.

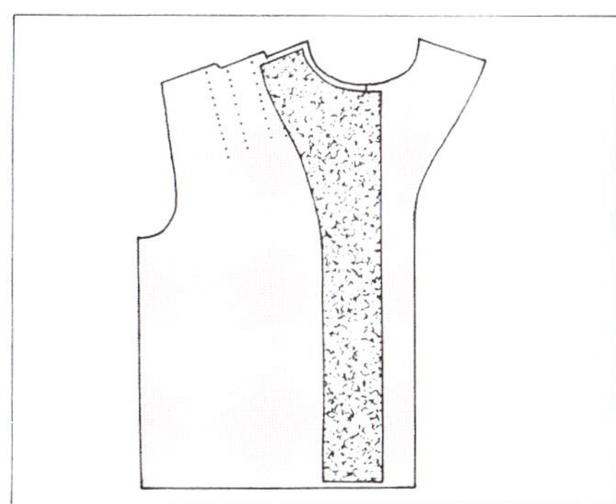

Make up the blouse following the instructions for basic blouse, page 43, but folding the attached facing to the wrong side before adding collar.
Use French seams, slit openings in the sleeves, hand worked or machine made buttonholes, and the Peter Pan collar. Attach the press stud to the top corner of the blouse under the collar.

French seam
This seam is suitable for all fine or fraying fabrics. It should be 5 mm (¼ in) wide when finished.
Place fabric pieces wrong side together, tack mid-way between raw edge and seam line i.e. about 5 mm (¼ in) from the edge.

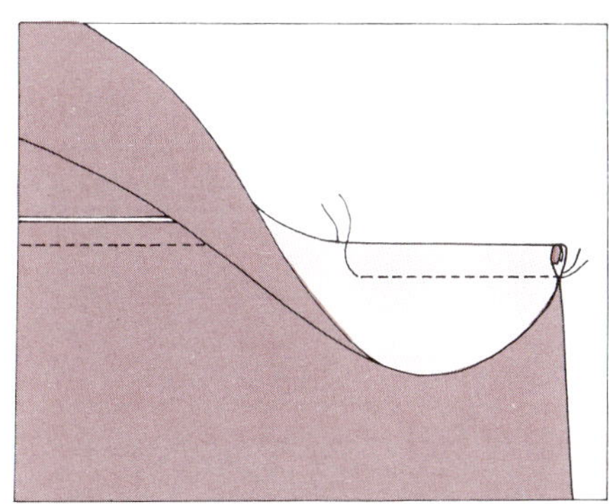

Machine with a straight stitch.
Remove tacks.
Press. Open the turnings with the toe of the iron, then press more firmly. Turn fabric over and press again to achieve a flat, straight seam. Do not overpress.
Trim the raw edges to 5 mm (¼ in), even less if the fabric is very fine.
With wrong side fabric outside, roll the seam between your fingers and hold it with the join exactly on the edge. Most fabrics will easily fall into this position having been pressed out. Some, like jersey, may have to be held quite firmly. Tack. Take one stitch below the edge, move the fingers to roll the next part of the seam, take one stitch and so on. Make sure the tacks go through the narrow edges inside the seam. Holding it up to light will show you exactly where to stitch in order to avoid the seam edge moving. Press the seam lightly.
The next row of stitching should fall on the seam line. Measure 5 mm (¼ in) from the edge and mark with tailor's chalk or a pin. Find a guide on your machine to use: most machines have one foot about that width from the needle to the outer edge. Some may have a groove on the needle plate to go by. You may be able to move the needle position to achieve the correct distance. Failing this, stick a piece of tape to the needle plate so that the inner edge forms a stitching guide. Machine the seam. Remove tacks. Press seam flat towards the back of the garment.

Peter Pan collar
Interface one collar piece, mark centre back.
Place collar pieces right sides together, tack and machine round outer edge. Remove tacks, trim and layer the raw edges and snip the edges at intervals of 5 mm (¼ in).

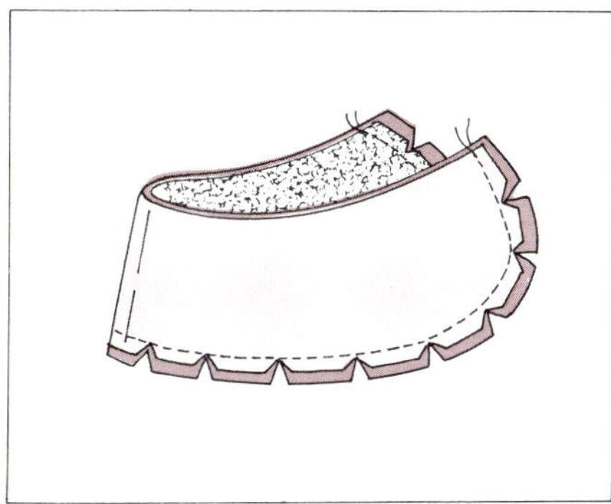

Turn collar right side out, roll to work the join to the edge and slightly to the underside and tack. Press the edge from both sides. Hold collar with interfaced side underneath and baste the raw edges together around the neck.

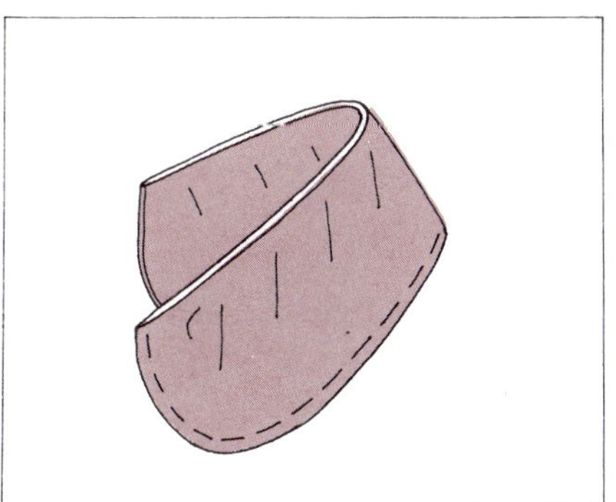

Place collar, interfaced side down to right side of blouse neck. Match centre back and insert vertical pin. Match collar ends to centre fronts and pin. Keep blouse on the table to avoid stretching the neck. Tack collar to neck edge, tacking from blouse side.

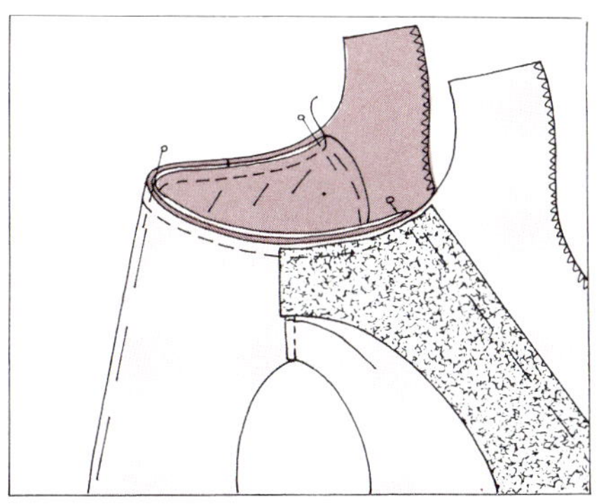

Fold over blouse facings on top of collar, match neck edges and tack. Machine from front edge of blouse through all layers as far as the shoulder seam of the blouse. Stitch from blouse side for accuracy. Snip tackings and remove from machined sections only.

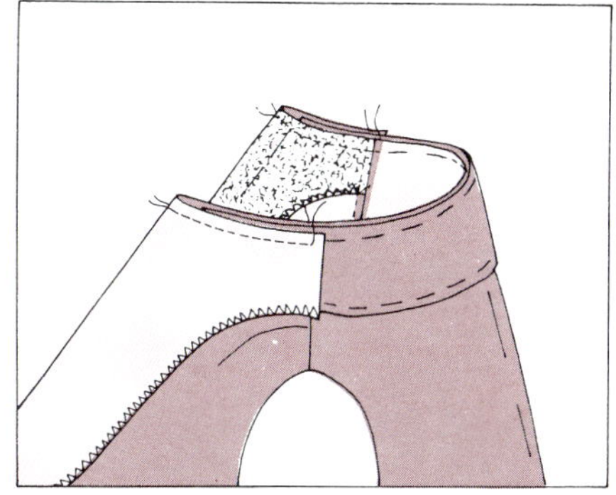

Cut a 2 cm (¾ in) wide bias strip of fabric, or a length of purchased binding long enough to fit across back neck. Press strip to remove the stretch. With bought binding press it to flatten out the creases a little. Fold over the blouse facing end and press. Place bias strip right side down on top of collar and extend at least 1 cm (⅜ in) over the facing. Place it so that it lies over the neck tacking but taking only 5 mm (¼ in) turning on the strip. Tack. Machine along strip overlapping machining at shoulder by 1 cm (⅜ in).

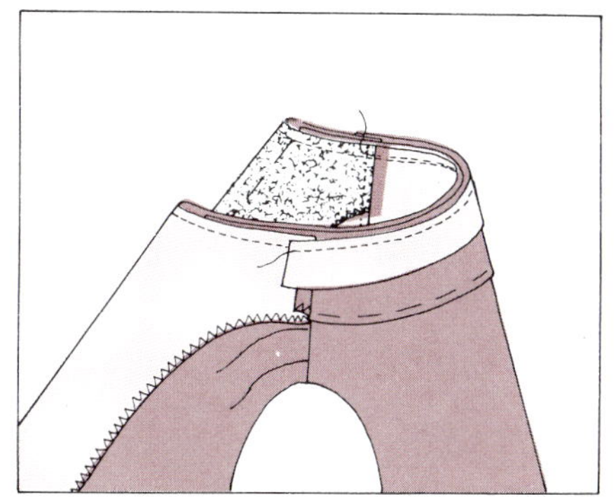

Trim and layer all neck, collar and facing edges. Snip all round the neck edge at intervals of 5 mm ($\frac{1}{4}$ in). Pull out the collar so that it extends upwards and ease downwards the facing, blouse and bias strip. Arrange on pressing surface and press the neck join carefully. Tack through all layers just below neck join, working from right side of blouse.

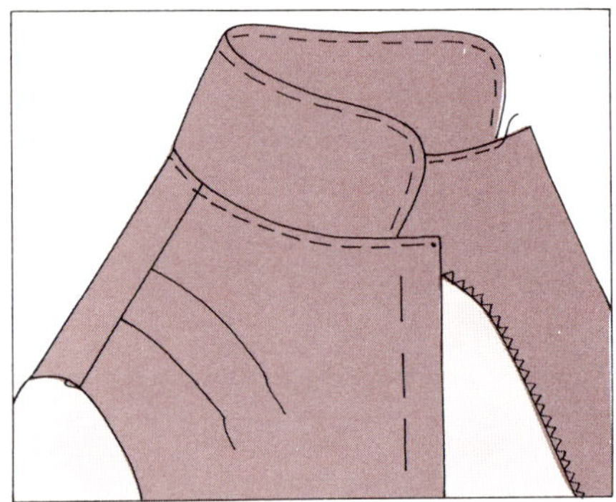

On the inside trim the raw edge of the bias strip to an even width, turn it under and tack down to blouse. The strip should be as narrow as possible when turned under. This will vary according to the fabric, for instance 5 mm ($\frac{1}{4}$ in) on crêpe de chine but 3 mm ($\frac{1}{8}$ in) on chiffon. Press then finish by working small slip-hemming stitches along edge of bias and also where facing runs along shoulder seam. Remove all tacking and press.

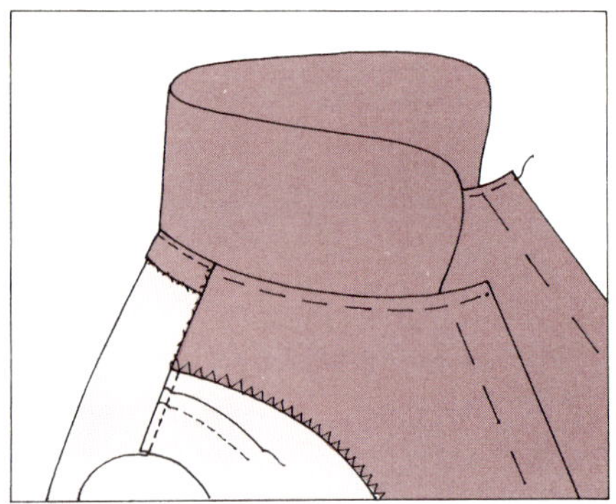

BLOUSE: BAND COLLAR

A short blouse with a narrow band collar which may be worn open to give a reveres effect. This short version of the pattern has optional patch pockets. We made it in a check cotton material and here it is worn with the panelled skirt (page 28).

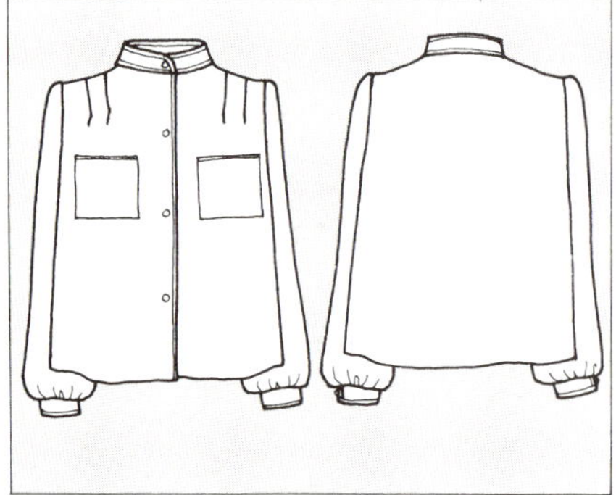

FABRIC

It can be made in plain or patterned fabrics such as cotton, polyester/cotton, seersucker, poplin, silk, voile, wool crêpe, shantung, slub silk, crinkle cotton, viyella.

Quantities

As for basic blouse (page 43). Interfacing is needed for front edges, collar, cuffs and pockets. Use light iron-on or sew-in interfacing.

HABERDASHERY

As for basic blouse (page 43), except that you need only 6 buttons.

PATTERN PIECES

17, 18, 19, 20, 21, 23, 28.

CUTTING OUT

Cut 21, 23 and 28 (pocket) in interfacing. Cut 20 in cuff interfacing.
Cut out 17, 18, 19, 21 in fabric. Leave 20, 23 pinned in place until required. Open out remaining fabric and press the pocket interfacing piece 28, to the wrong side of the fabric.

Marking
Mark fold line on pockets. Mark tucks, openings, centre front and sleeve head on blouse pieces.

MAKING UP

Attach interfacing and insert tucks, tack and fit as for basic blouse.

Patch pockets (optional)
After fitting, remove tacking from side seams, make and attach pockets. Place interfaced pockets right sides together and using tracing wheel and carbon paper, rule lines across the bottom of the pocket and up the sides exactly 1.5cm ($\frac{5}{8}$in) in from the edge. Rule a line exactly across the corner – it may help to crease the fabric first.

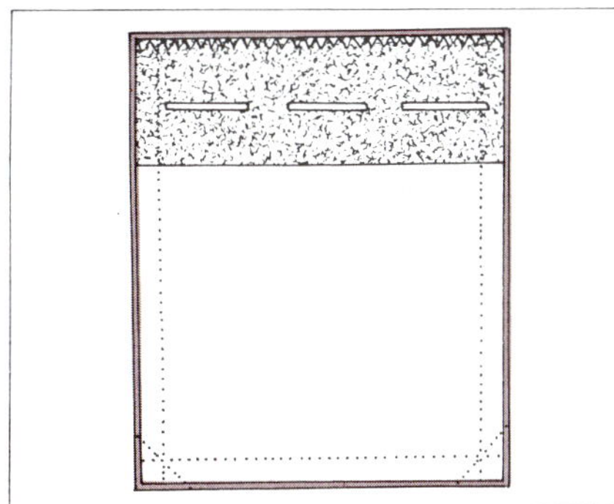

Press interfacing strip across the top of the pocket with edges level and press. Neaten the top edge of the pocket with zig-zag stitch. Fold the top of the pocket over on to the right side and machine across the ends on the marked line. Fold up the corners at the bottom until the diagonal marks and pocket edges are level. Machine across the corner to form a mitre.

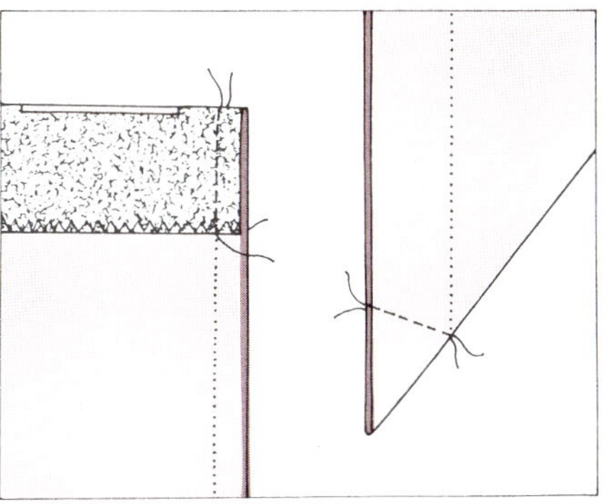

Cut off the surplus fabric at the mitres and at the top. Turn pocket right side out and press all edges.

Stitch shoulder tucks.
Pin pocket to blouse front. Adjust pocket position to a flattering level and mark the position with a pin. Place both blouse fronts together and work a row of tailor tacks to indicate the position of the top of each pocket. Place pockets in position, tack across the top and baste down the centre. Tack round the outer edge.

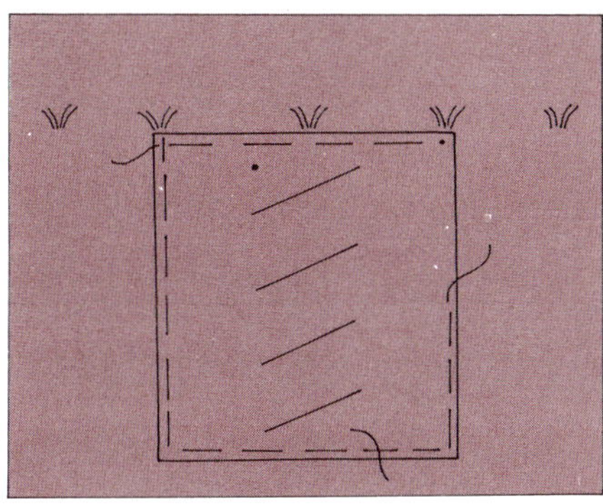

Attach by hand-working small catch stitch under the edge, or machine round the edge, stitching a rectangle or triangle at the top corners.
Stitch and finish side seams as for basic blouse (page 43).

Band collar
Attach interfacing to wrong side of fabric. Cut out collar, cut another collar piece without interfacing. Mark centre back fold on both pieces.
Attach interfacing to wrong side of blouse fronts. Neaten outer edge and end of facing and attach it to blouse by machining 1.5cm ($\frac{5}{8}$in) from edge.

Press this join open then trim the raw edges to 5mm ($\frac{1}{4}$in).

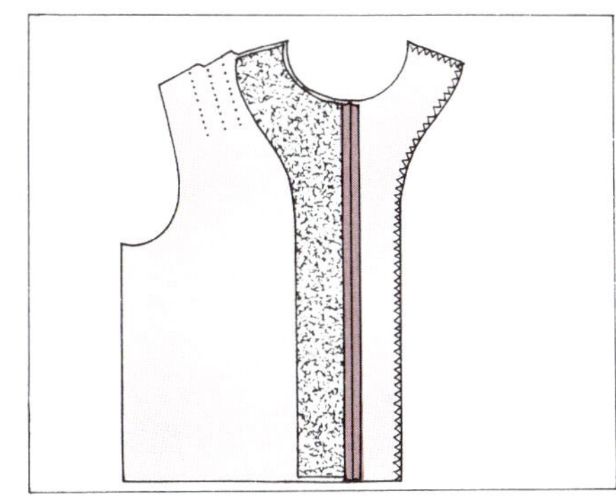

Join and finish shoulder seams. Fold front facing to inside of blouse, tack the centre front edge with the join on the edge. Press. Hold the facing back with basting. Slip pieces of adhesive web underneath to keep it in position.

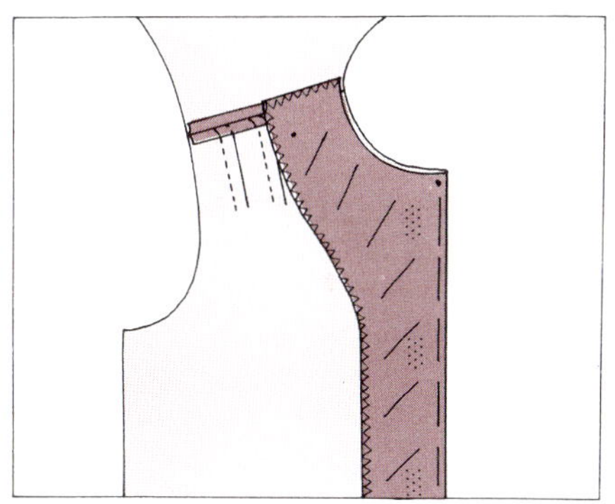

Place interfaced collar to blouse. Machine with right sides together matching centre back marks. Pin, inserting the pins vertically. If necessary snip the blouse neck edge so that it meets the collar edge more easily. There should be 1.5cm ($\frac{5}{8}$in) of collar extending beyond the centre front faced edges.

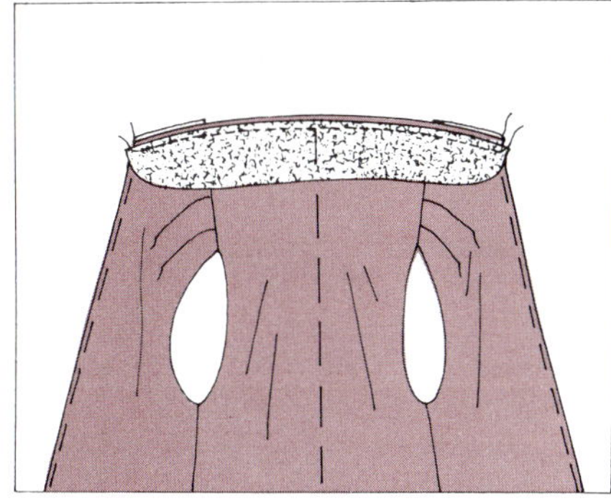

Machine collar to blouse. Remove tackings, trim the turnings down to 5mm ($\frac{1}{4}$in) or less, snip well and press so that the collar stands upright.
Place second collar piece against first, right sides together, and match centre back marks. Baste together along the middle of the collar then tack round the outer edge. Machine accurately taking the correct seam allowance and starting and finishing

the machining exactly where the neck stitching ends.

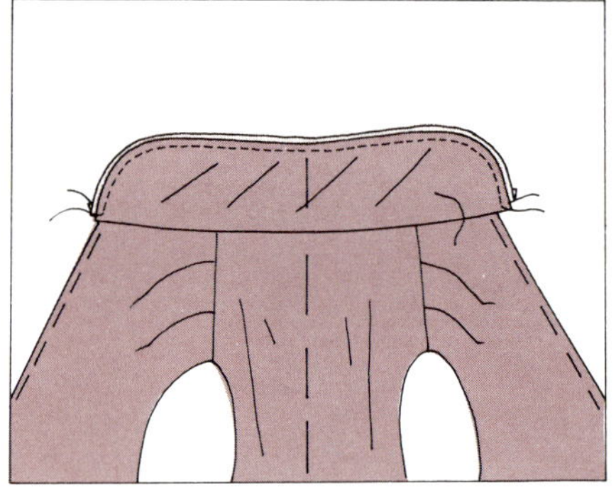

Trim the turnings to 3mm (⅛in) and snip all round the outer edge of the collar.
Remove all tackings. Turn collar right side out, rolling the edge until the join is precisely on the edge. Tack near the join, smooth the collar pieces together and baste from end to end of the collar.

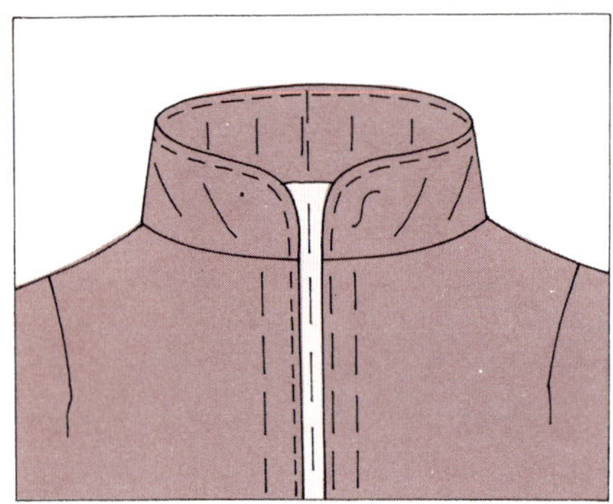

On the inside, trim the remaining raw edge of collar, cutting off 1cm (⅜in). Turn this edge under and tack it down so that it lies on the machine stitching. Finish by working very small hemming stitches between the collar edge and the machine stitches. Attach the shoulder end of the facing to the shoulder seam with a few herringbone or hemming stitches. Remove all tackings and press.

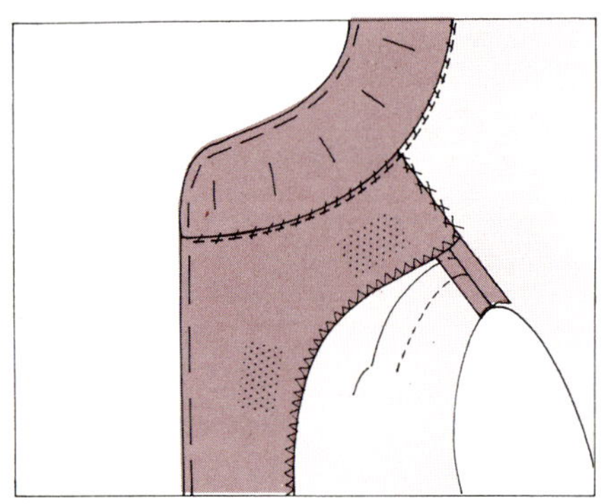

Buttons

Space out 4 buttons on the blouse with the top one at chest level, the next at bust line level.

Finish the rest of the blouse as for the basic blouse (page 46).

FRILLED BLOUSE

This version is a romantic blouse with a band collar. Flattering double frills are set into the cuffs and around the collar. It can be made in a wide variety of fabrics either crisp or soft. The version above, teamed with the pleated skirt (page 33), is in white spotted cotton voile and we have added a pretty neck tie (optional).

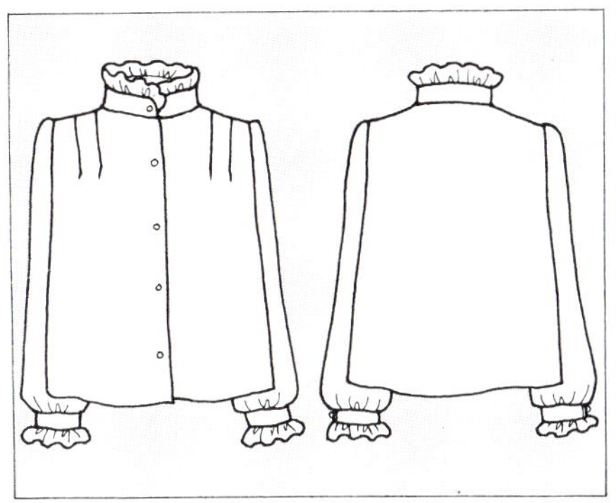

FABRIC

Suitable fabrics are: crêpe de chine, synthetic crêpe, pongée, georgette, chiffon, taffeta, voile, lamé, peau de soie, spun silk, moss crêpe, polyester cotton, lawn, crinkle cotton.

Quantities
As for the basic blouse (page 43), but using the following additional amount for frills.

Width	*Quantity*
90cm (36in)	35cm
115cm (45in)	25cm

Interfacing is needed for neck band, front edges and cuffs. Use light iron-on or sew-in variety.

HABERDASHERY

As for basic blouse, page 43.

PATTERN PIECES

17, 18, 19, 20, 21, 23, 26, 27.

CUTTING OUT

Cut 21 and 23 in interfacing. Mark seam allowance all round collar, 23. Pin all pieces except 20 on to fabric and cut out 17, 18, 19, 21, leaving the others until needed. Do not cut cuffs yet.
Press interfacing to wrong sides of blouse fronts.

MAKING UP

Follow instructions for basic blouse (page 43), except for collar, cuffs and optional neck tie.

Frilled collar
The frill is a straight piece of fabric folded double and inserted in the join of the collar. It is very full when gathered and in medium weight or

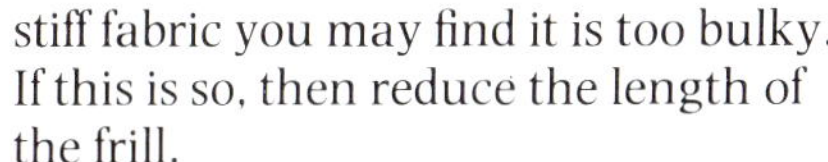

stiff fabric you may find it is too bulky. If this is so, then reduce the length of the frill.
The frill can follow the top edge of the collar round the curve to the neck join (graded frill), or it can end vertically above the centre front line (straight end frill, see photograph page 35).
The cuff frills can be varied in the same way.
Interface one piece of collar and attach it to the neckline. Trim and snip the turnings and press them up into the collar.

Attaching graded frill
Fold neck frill in half right side out and press. Mark the centre. Insert a gathering thread 1.5cm ($\frac{5}{8}$in) from the raw edgs, running it down to the fold for the 8–10cm (3–4in) near the corners.

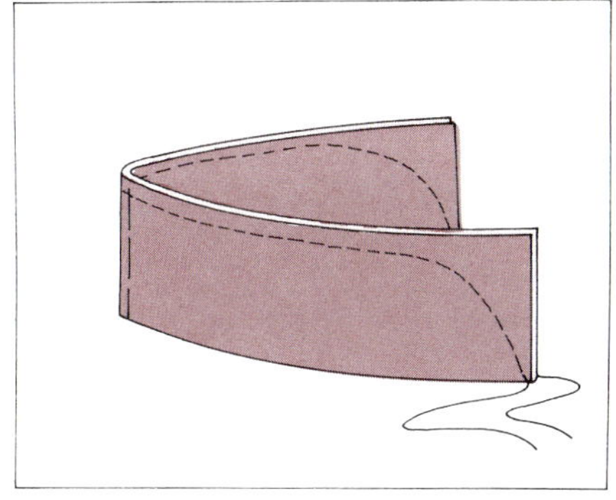

Cut off the surplus at the corner. Place frill to right side of collar. Pin middle of frill at centre back of collar and pin the ends to the corners of the collar. Pull up the gathering thread until the frill fits the collar. Wind the thread ends round a pin to hold. Even out the gathers and pin frequently round the collar.

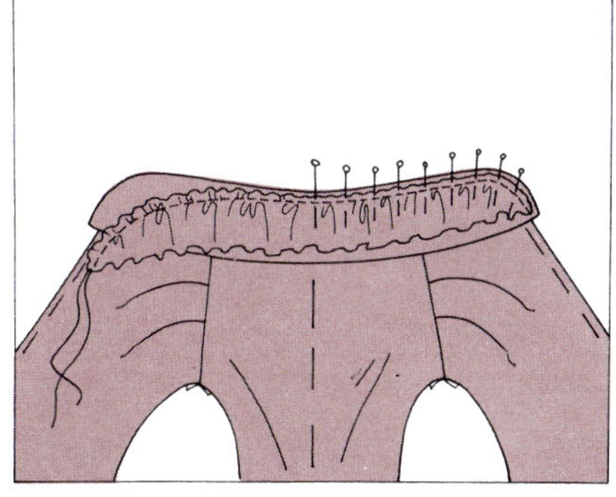

Tack on the gathers exactly on the seam line of the collar. Remove all pins. Machine frill to collar, keeping gathers as even as possible. Remove tacking, remove gathering thread. Trim down frill edge to 5mm ($\frac{1}{4}$in). Place second collar piece on top of frill, right side down and tack down. Turn collar over and machine round outer edge following the line of machining attaching the frill. Remove tacking.

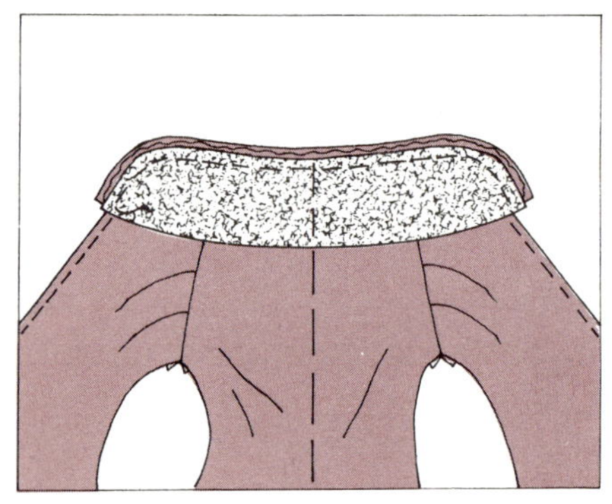

Trim the turnings to 5mm (¼in) or less in fine fabric. Snip the turnings well. Roll collar right side out so that frill stands up, smooth down both parts of collar, tack round outer edge just below join and also baste along the length of the collar.

On the inside trim 1cm (⅜in) off the raw edge of the collar, turn it under, tack on to the neck join stitching and hem neatly picking up each machine stitch. Remove all tackings and press collar but not frill.

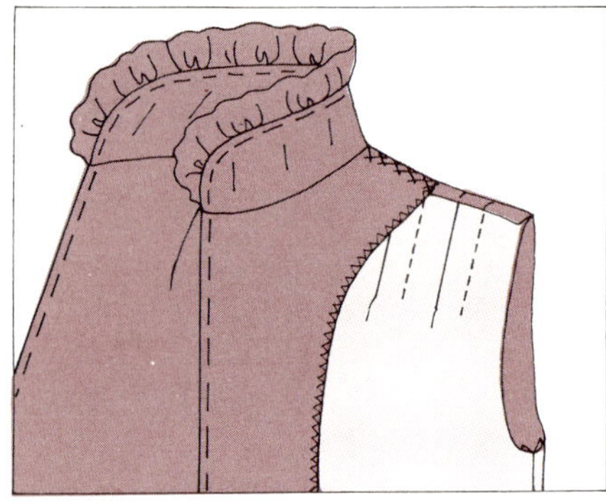

Straight end frill

Fold frill ends right sides together. Machine across ends, trim, turn right side out; fold frill and press to mark the middle. Insert a gathering thread along the raw edges.

Complete the collar as described above for the graded frill.

Sleeves with frilled cuffs

Make faced slit openings in sleeves (see page 45). Stitch the sleeve seams. Insert gathering thread round cuff end.

Cut out cuffs.

The cuff will need a join along the outer edge so fold under 4cm (1½in) along one edge of the cuff pattern to reduce it to half width including seam allowances. Cut out in light iron-on interfacing. Mark the extension and also mark an even 1.5cm (⅝in) seam allowance all round, using tracing wheel and carbon paper.

Open out remaining fabric and press interfacing to wrong side making sure straight grain is correct. Cut round interfacing. Cut two more identical cuff pieces in fabric.

Attach cuffs.

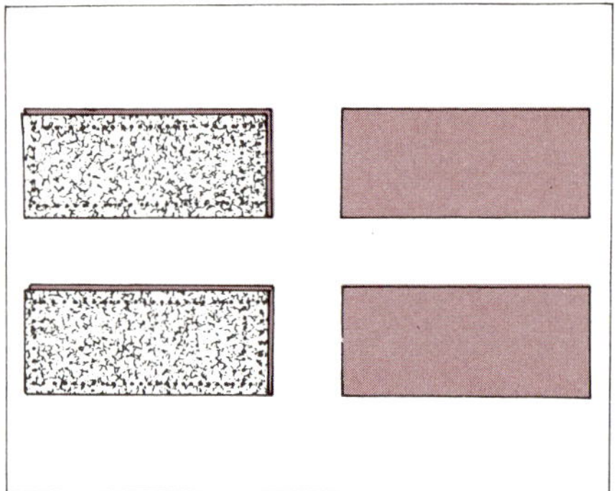

Pin interfaced cuffs to sleeves, pull up gathers and tack on the seam lines. Machine with gathers uppermost. Remove tackings and gathers. Trim down the raw edges to 5mm (¼in) or less. Press them into the cuff.

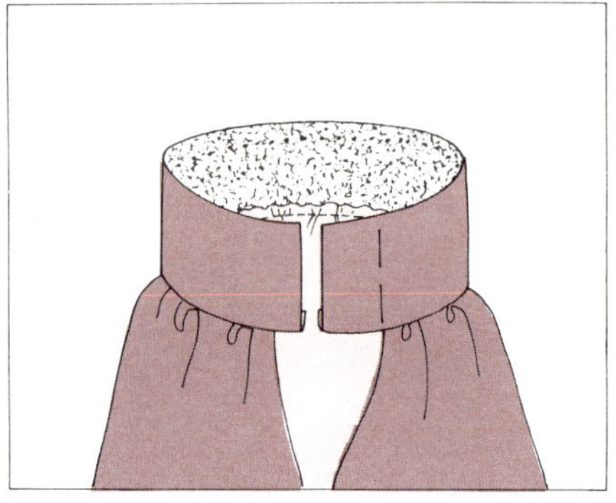

Frills

Fold each frill piece in half. For a graded frill press with right side out. For a frill with a straight end, fold right sides together, stitch across the ends, trim, turn right side out and then press. Insert gathering threads as described for neck frill. Place frill to right side of cuff with ends of frill to ends of cuff. The frill with straight ends should finish level with the seam line at the end of the cuff. The graded frill is taken round the corner to the sleeve edge. Make sure the ends of the frill are positioned accurately and pin. Pull up the gathers, anchor the thread ends by winding them round a pin.

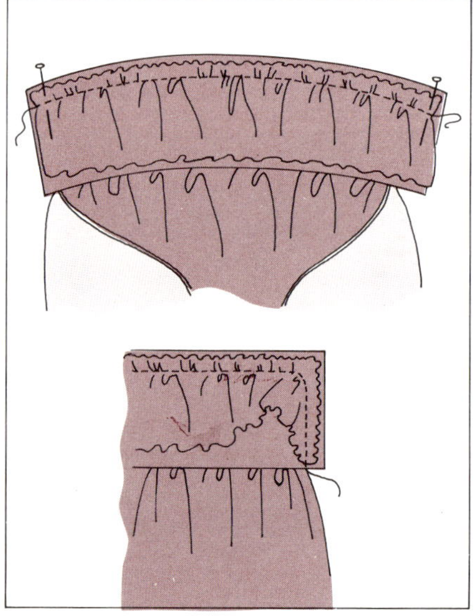

Even out the gathers and pin frill to cuff. Tack exactly on the marked seam line and machine all round outer edge to attach frill from the edge of the wrist opening.

Place second piece of cuff on top right side down. Tack, machine across cuff end, along the length, across the other end and along the extension. Fasten off thread ends. Remove tackings. Trim edges to 5mm (¼in) or less, cut off corners.

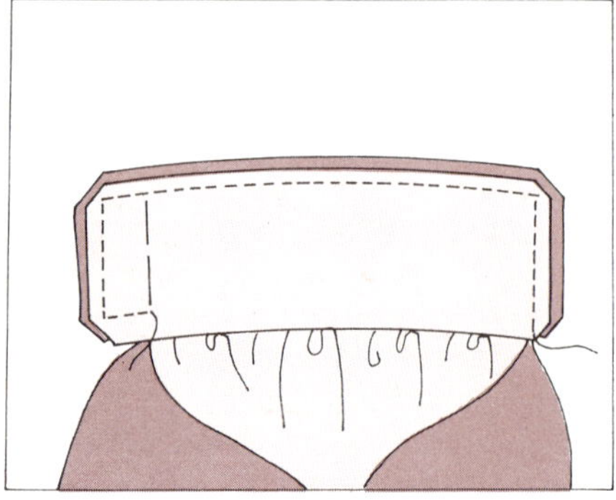

Turn cuff right side out, pulling frill out. Smooth down both parts of the cuff and tack round the edge. Press the cuff without crushing the frill. On the inside trim the remaining raw edge, turn it under so that the edge falls on the machine stitching. Tack and hem into the machine stitches. Remove tackings.

Make buttonholes in the cuffs in the usual way.

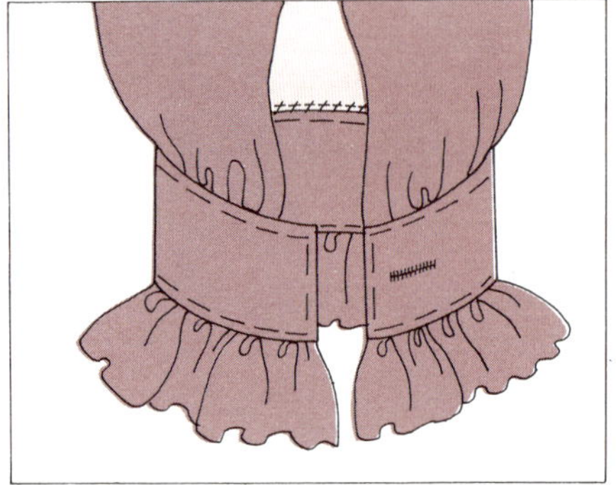

Neck tie (optional)

Cut two strips of fabric 75cm × 8cm (30in × 3in) on the straight grain. Machine one pair of short ends right sides together. Press join. Cut a piece of lightweight, iron-on interfacing 33cm × 2.5cm (13in × 1in) and mark the centre. Match mark to centre join of fabric and iron interfacing to centre section 5mm (¼in) from one long edge.

Fold band lengthways right sides together and machine all round taking 5mm (¼in) seam allowance. The short ends may be sloped. Leave a gap and turn tie to right side. Press. Slip stitch gap, top stitch all round, press again.

Left: round neck blouse (page 57) in striped cotton, worn over camisole (page 68) and knee-length shorts (page 66) in pink towelling.

Inset: the pink towelling camisole and shorts; sports shorts (page 67) in navy stretch towelling, worn with the camisole in navy and white striped cotton jersey.

Page 56: coat (page 22) made in green showerproof gabardine and lined with a toning check Viyella.

BLOUSE: ROUND NECK

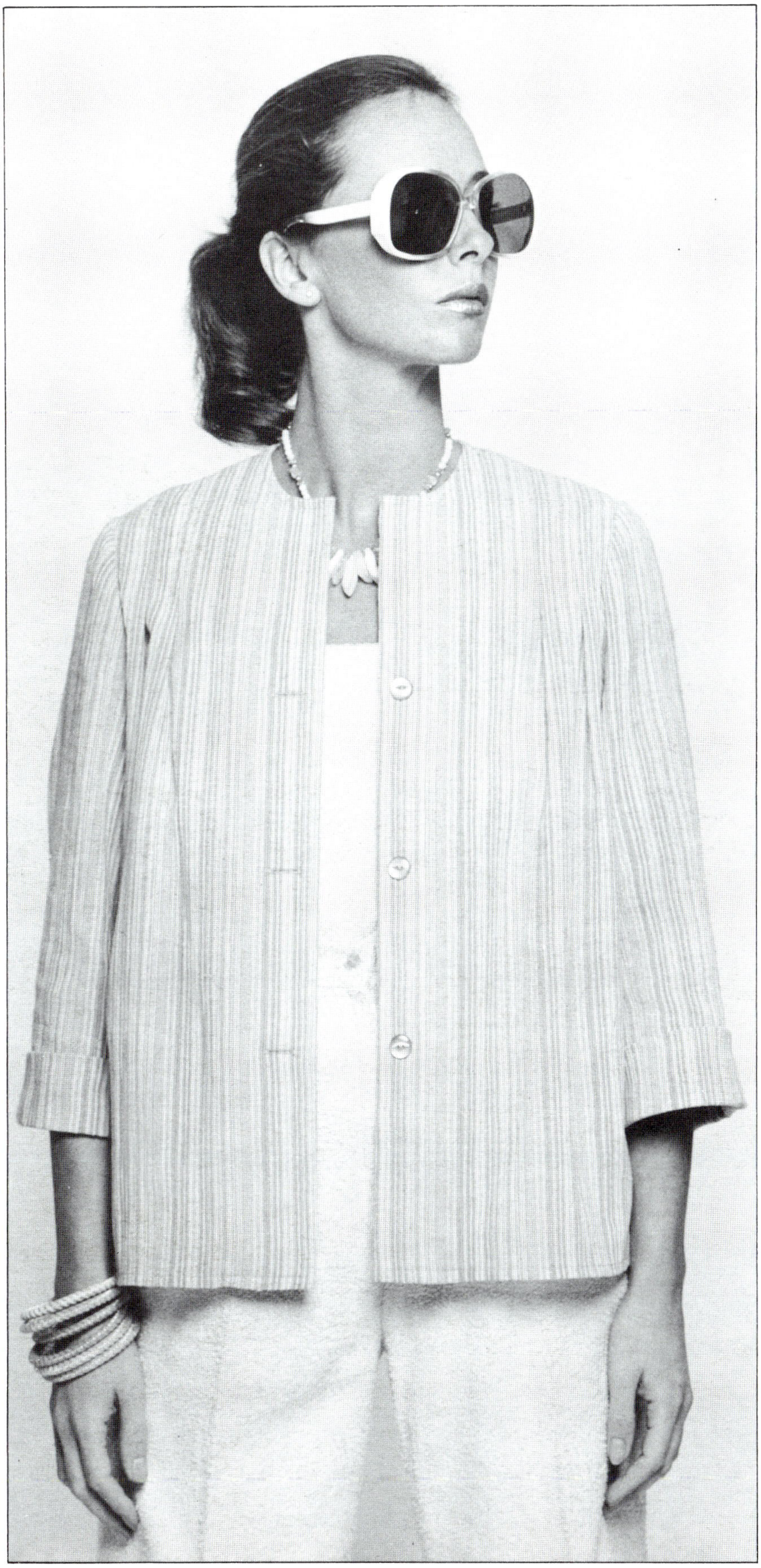

Casual style blouse with round neck; three quarter sleeves may be plain or have turn-back cuff. May be worn tunic style and belted or tucked in.

FABRICS

Use crisp fabrics such as cotton, polyester/cotton, poplin, crêpon, seersucker, Madras or soft cotton jersey. We used striped cotton.

Quantities
As for basic blouse (page 43). Interfacing is needed for front edges and front and back neckline. Use a light iron-on or sew-in variety. Finished lengt back neck to hem size 12: 61 cm (24 in).

HABERDASHERY

2 reels thread

Interfacing (see above)

Cuff interfacing

3 small buttons

Adhesive web for buttonholes

An adjustable marker helps to space buttons accurately

PATTERN PIECES

17, 18, 19, 21, 22. Pin together 21 and 18 and cut out as one piece as described for Peter Pan collar blouse, page 48.

MAKING UP

Follow instructions for basic blouse but finish neckline with facings. If you want a plain sleeve hem, the sleeve can be cut shorter and a narrow machined or a deeper hand-stitched hem can be used. Alternatively, make a turn-back cuff.
Space out the three buttons with one at chest level, one above the waist and the third mid-way between.

Neck facings
Attach interfacing to wrong side of back neck as well as fronts. Fold front facing back on to right side of blouse, insert a few pins near the fold. Baste round the neckline.

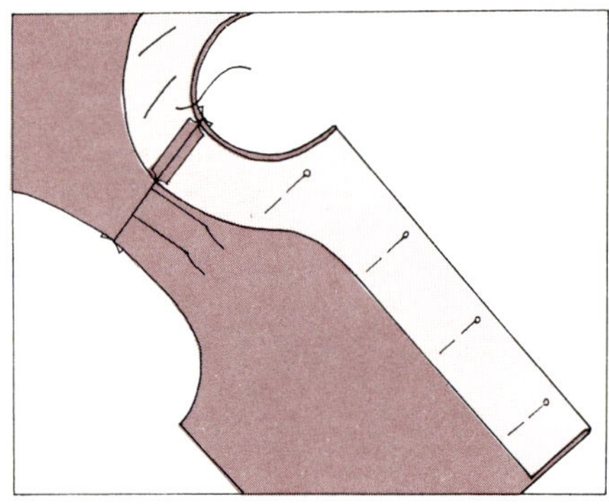

Place back neck facing to right side of back neck of blouse and baste.
Press back the two ends of facing so that they meet at the shoulder point. Make a join, using the creases as a stitching guide line. Trim raw edges down to 5 mm ($\frac{1}{4}$ in).
Machine round the neck taking 1.5 cm ($\frac{5}{8}$ in) seam allowance. Trim the raw edges to 3 mm ($\frac{1}{8}$ in), cut off corners, snip well towards the stitching. Remove pins and tacking. Press the stitching flat. Trim the outer edge of the facing neatly, and then overcast or zig-zag.

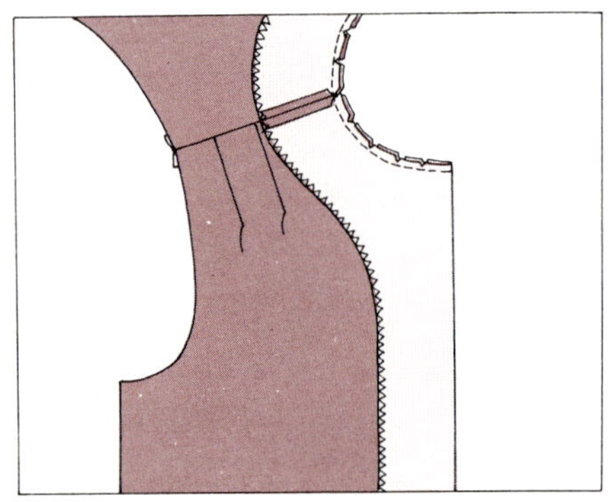

Run the toe of the iron under the facing, pushing into the neck join. Roll the facing completely to the inside of the blouse.
Tack and press the edge. On the inside hold the facings to the shoulder seams with herringbone stitch and slip a few pieces of adhesive web under the facing down the front and across the back neck. Press well.

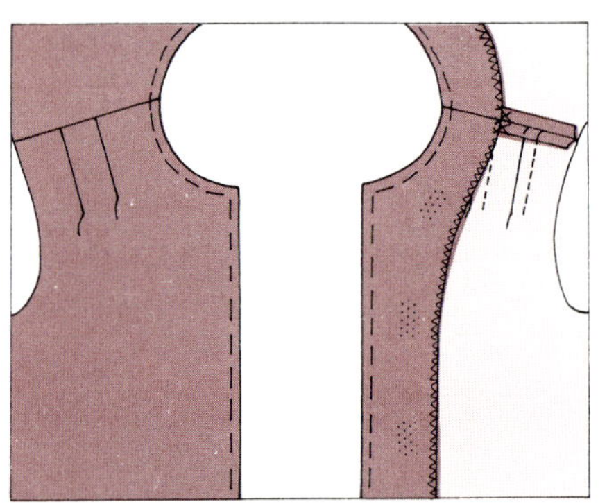

Turn-back cuff
If the fabric is very soft, attach a strip of interfacing to the sleeve on the wrong side before sewing the sleeve seam. The interfacing should be at least 10 cm (4 in) deep. After stitching the seam, neaten the lower edge of the sleeve and catch in the interfacing.

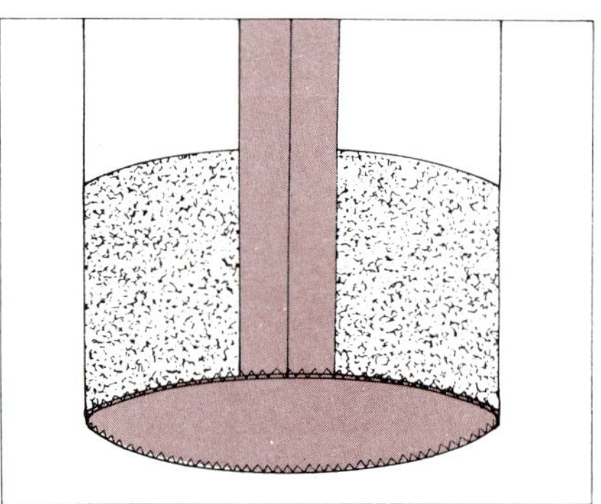

Fold up the bottom of the sleeve to the wrong side to a depth of 10 cm (4 in), press and hold down the neatened edge with catch stitch.

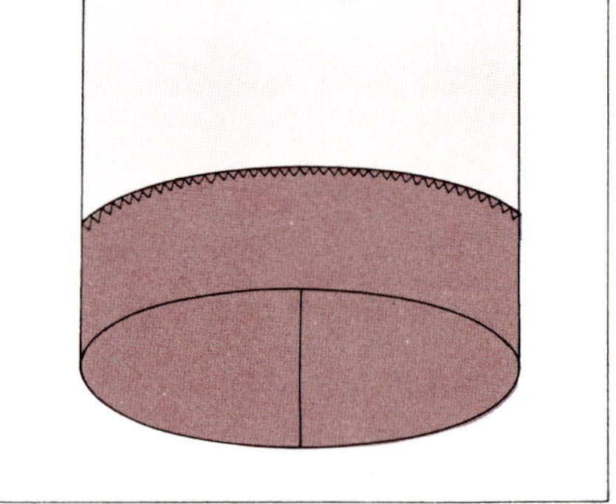

Fold up the sleeve on to the right side to a depth of 5 cm (2 in) to form a cuff and press.

TROUSERS

Classic trousers with straight legs, deep front waist pleats, slanting inset pockets, front fly zip and waistband. There are optional patch pockets on the back.

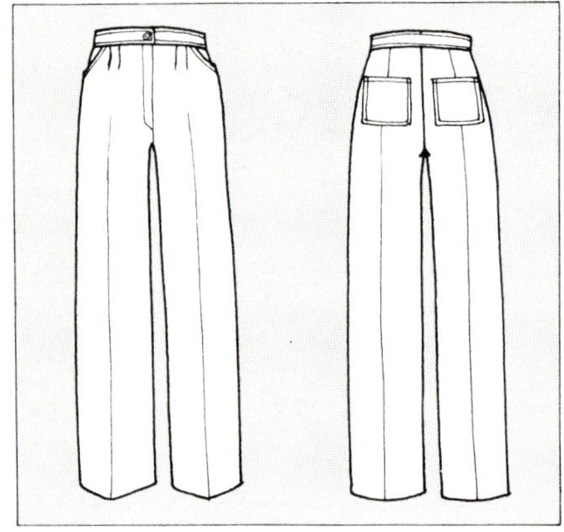

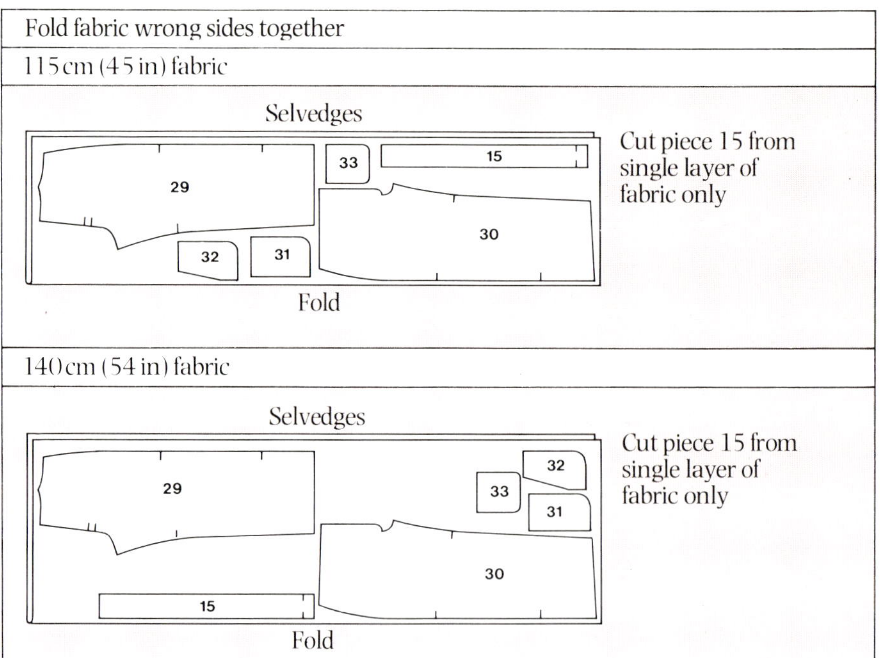

FABRIC

These trousers can be made in any fabric to team or mix with any of the other patterns in the book. Try them in flannel, corduroy, velvet, gaberdine, denim, silk or synthetic jersey, cotton drill or satin.
Photographs on page 38 and the back cover show the trousers made in black French jersey and white cotton sailcloth with matching jacket.

Quantities

Width	*Size*	*Quantity*
115cm (45in)	10	2.30m
	12	2.30m
	14	2.30m
	16	2.30m
	18	2.35m
140cm (54in)	10	1.85m
	12	1.90m
	14	2.20m
	16	2.30m
	18	2.35m

Interfacing is needed for the waistband.
Attach light iron-on interfacing to the pocket facing piece and fly.
If using heavy fabric, reduce bulk by cutting the pocket facing from lining material. Insert band interfacing in the back pocket. On light, soft fabrics the back pocket should also have lightweight interfacing attached.
Transparent fabrics like chiffon or thin fabrics in pale colours, e.g. crêpe, will need mounting or lining. Use the same quantity as for the fabric.
Finished length inside leg: 76cm (30in).
Finished width at ankle, size 12: 53cm (21in).

HABERDASHERY

- 2 reels thread
- Iron-on interfacing for pockets
- Waistband interfacing
- 20cm (8in) nylon, metal or jeans zip
- Waistband fastening: 1 button or trouser clip or Velcro
- Adhesive hemming web (for firm fabrics)
- Short piece of seam tape for crutch seam
- Length of band interfacing for back pockets

PATTERN PIECES

29, 30, 31, 32, 33 and 15.
Begin by comparing the crutch depth and leg length at inside seam with your own measurements. The finished length and width will depend on how you intend to accessorise the outfit but also on the type of fabric used and on your figure. If you prefer the trousers tapered, gently slope the outside and inside leg seams by equal amounts from thigh to hem. This can be done at the fitting stage or on the pattern pieces. If you are uncertain of the amount of adjustment to make, it may help to measure up a pair of your own trousers that fit well. Be cautious at first: even 1 cm ($\frac{1}{2}$in) reduction on each side can make a big difference to the finished effect.

CUTTING OUT

Cut 32, pocket bag, in iron-on interfacing.
Pin all pattern pieces in position on fabric and cut out 30 and 31. Do not cut 15, (waistband) until required.
Open out the remaining fabric. Press 32, pocket interfacing pieces, to the wrong side of the fabric and cut out. If the fabric is bulky use lining fabric for this piece instead of fabric. Cut out back pockets 33 or, if interfacing, cut that, press to wrong side of fabric and cut out.

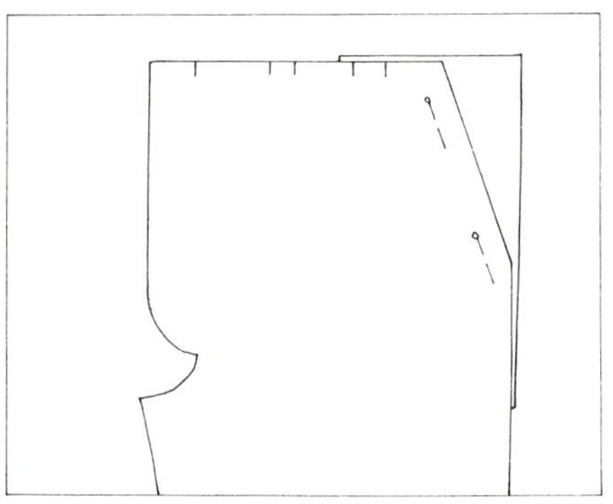

Marking
Mark centre front zip base point. Cut off left side extension of fabric as indicated on the pattern.
Mark darts and pocket position on back. Mark pleats and balance marks on trouser fronts. Mark the balance mark on the outside leg edge, above hemline on back and front.
The back pockets may be left off although they may be an advantage in 'breaking up' the seat area.
The front inset pockets may be omitted. Do this if you feel the extra bulk of the pockets in addition to the deep pleats at the front, is going to be too bulky on your figure. Also, omitting the inset pockets will enable you to put the zip in the left side seam if you prefer. The decision will depend on the fabric, the particular outfit and your own figure.
To remove the inset pockets pin together the front trouser pattern, 30, and the pocket pattern, 31, matching

the balance marks at the waist and overlapping the pieces. Place this on the fabric and cut out in fabric in the usual way.
If the trousers need lining, cut out the lining by assembling the front pattern, 30, without pockets as described above. Cut out this piece and 29 in lining. Make the two legs in lining, and insert inside the fabric legs and baste together round the waist. Join crutch seam, insert zip, attach waist-band. Turn up hems separately.

MAKING UP

1 Inset trouser pockets

Place the interfaced pocket bag pieces to right side of trouser front right sides together, edges meeting and tack, taking 1.5cm ($\frac{5}{8}$in) seam allowance. Machine. Trim the edges to 5mm ($\frac{1}{4}$in) and press the turnings open.

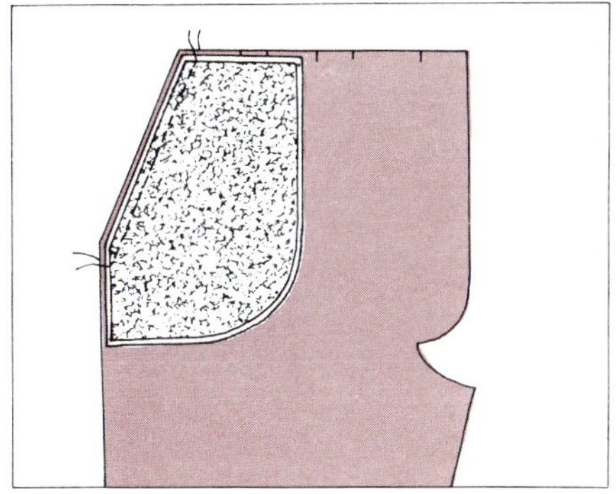

Roll the pocket bag piece to the wrong side. Work out the edge until the join is on the edge. Tack below the edge and press. Work a row of top stitching close to the edge.
Place the trouser pocket piece under the bag area right side up, matching the balance mark at the waistline and baste through all layers to hold.

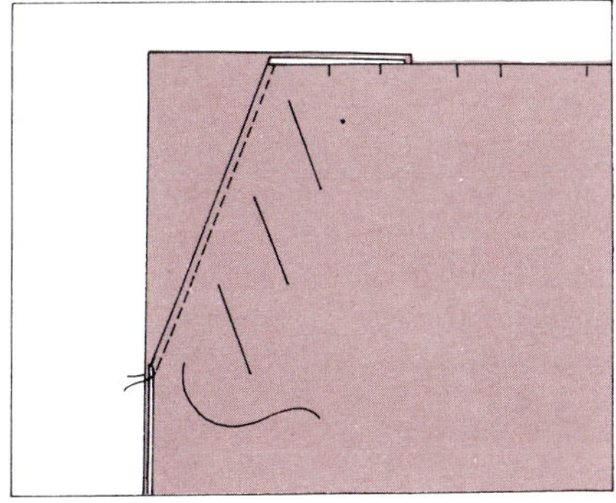

Turn the trousers wrong side up and draw a neat line the shape of the bag on the upper layer with chalk or chalk pencil. Machine through the two layers on the line to form the bag. Trim off the surplus fabric edges to within 5mm ($\frac{1}{4}$in) of the machining (less on fine fabric) with zig-zag or overcasting.

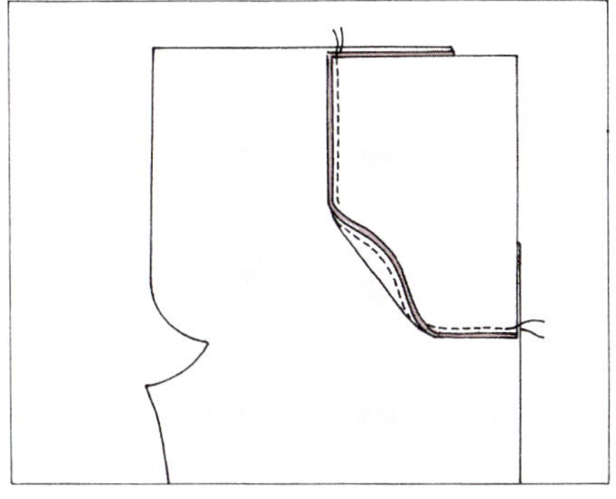

2 Darts

Fold one back trouser leg with right side inside, match the dart markings and insert two pins across the dart. Tack from waist to dart point. Remove pins. Press the dart using light pressure to flatten it. The bulk of the dart should be towards the waist.
Fit the dart by putting this back leg over your bottom, holding the waist edge to your waist line. The shape created at the point of the dart should be sufficient for your figure and the dart should be long enough to produce the shaping at the right level for you. If you have low buttocks insert a pin to lengthen the dart a little. If the dart is too long, snip the tacking and shorten it. If you need more shaping, make the dart deeper at the waist but running to the original point position. Finally, if you have a thick waist or a flat bottom, reduce the width and length of the dart.
If you usually experience difficulty in fitting the back waist darts of trousers re-tack and leave them tacked until the whole leg is fitted, otherwise proceed to the next stage. Remember that the fitting of the waist is done at a later stage using the side seams and front tucks as adjustment points.
Machine the darts from waist to point, fastening off the thread ends securely. Remove tackings. Press the darts so that the bulk lies towards the centre back seam. Press on the wrong side and again on the right side.

3 Back pockets (optional)

These are patch pockets to be machined on to the outside of the trousers over the darts. Place a length of band interfacing, lightest weight, on the wrong side of each pocket, with the edge level with the pocket edge. Press in position. If you have attached interfacing to the pocket, the banding should be put on top of it. Neaten the pocket top edge with zig-zag stitch. Fold over the edge to the right side on the perforations in the banding. Press. Machine across the end taking 1.5cm ($\frac{5}{8}$in) seam allowance. Trim ends and cut off the corners.
Turn this top edge over to wrong side of the pocket and press. Fold in and

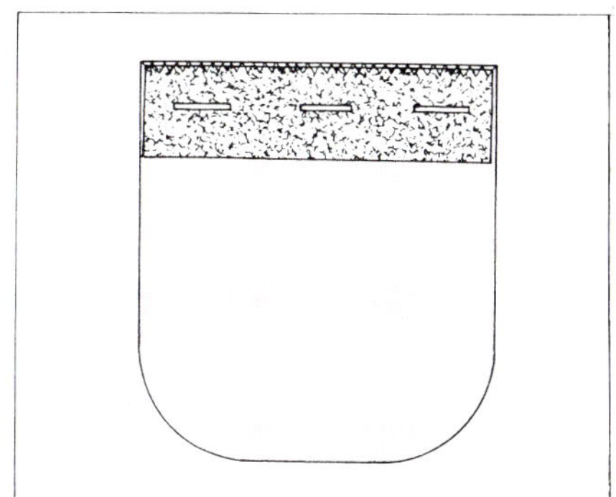

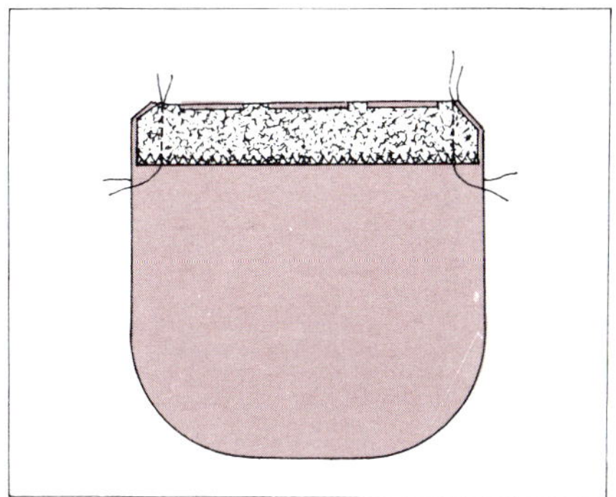

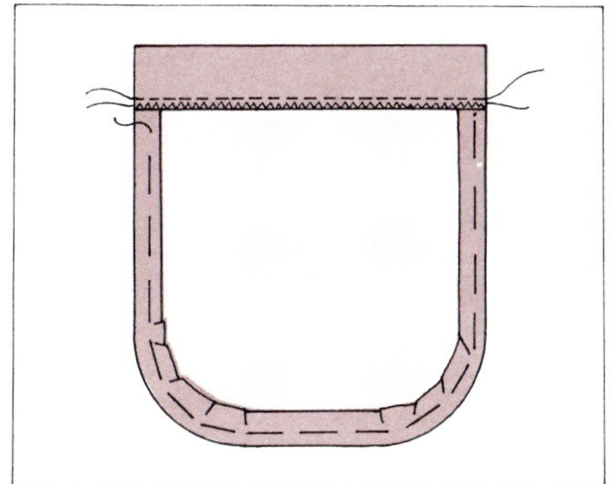

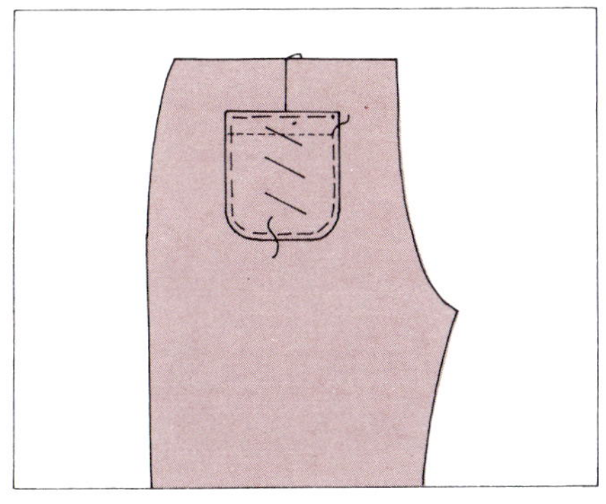

tack the outer curved edge of the pocket taking 1.5cm ($\frac{5}{8}$in) seam allowance and press. Work a row of machining across the top edge just above the neatening and, if you wish, another near the top of the pocket. On the wrong side trim the raw edge round the curve to 5mm ($\frac{1}{4}$in) and on bulky fabrics snip the remainder so that it lies flat.
Place each pocket in position on the right side of the trouser legs matching the top to the marked line. Tack along the top and then baste down the middle. Tack round the outer edge to hold the pockets in position.
Machine round the outside edge, work a triangle or rectangle at each top

corner. A second row may be added inside the first. Fasten off thread ends. Remove all tackings and press.

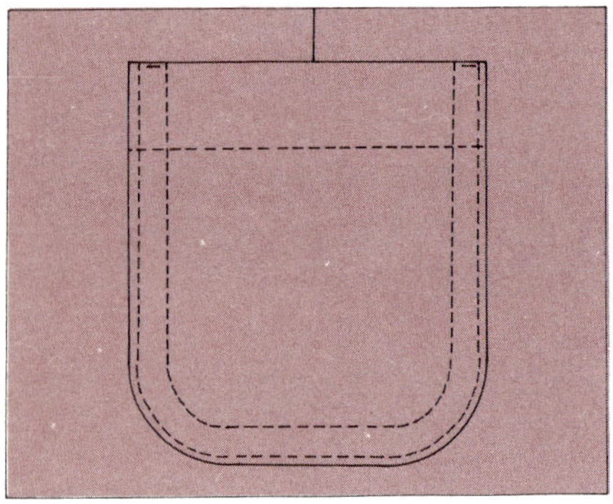

4 Leg seams
Place one back leg on the table, right side up, with the front leg piece on top, right side down, and with side seam edges level and balance marks matching. Tack from hem to waist taking 1.5cm ($\frac{5}{8}$in) seam allowance and tacking through the pocket bag when you reach it.

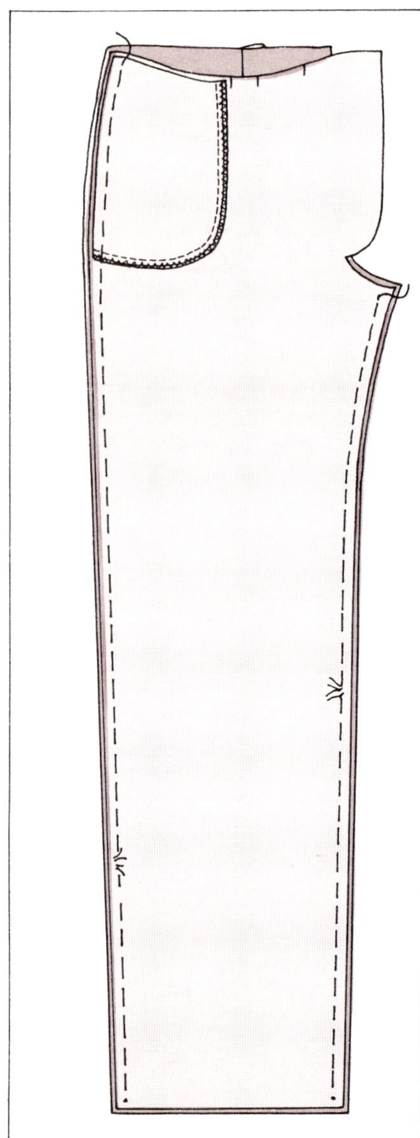

Lift the top layer of fabric in order to bring together the edges of the fabric

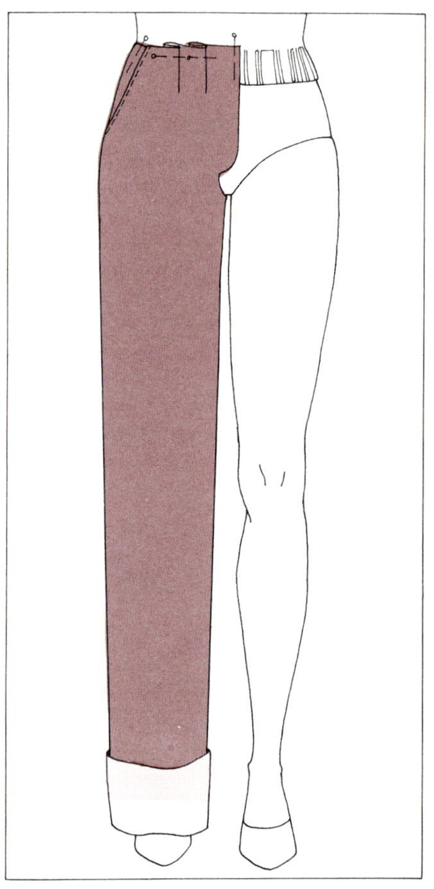

at the inside leg seam position. Tack from hem to crutch taking 1.5cm ($\frac{5}{8}$in) seam allowance.
Turn the leg right side out and try it on. Wear a jumper and pin the trouser waist to the jumper to hold it firm. At the hem turn up the surplus length on to the outside.
Pin at side, centre back and centre front and fold over the tucks at the front waist and pin them. Check the width of the leg at hemline, knee and thigh level, pinning up to take out surplus width or snipping the tacking to let out if it is too tight at thigh level. Take off the trouser leg and re-tack the seams if necessary. Tack up the second leg to correspond. With the legs right side out, insert a second row of tacking near the seam line on the outside leg with the seam turnings pressed towards the back of the trouser.
Tack the two legs together for the next fitting of the legs. Hold legs right side out and put the two inside leg seams together. Pin.
Tack from the crutch point up to back waist and then from the crutch up to the zip base point.
Turn up the hems to approximately the level you established at the previous fitting; tack near the fold and baste the surplus to the leg to hold it up out of the way ready to fit.
Tack across the front tucks and remove the pins. Fold under the fly extension on the right front and tack.
Fit Put on the trousers; put shoes on; pin together the front opening. Pass

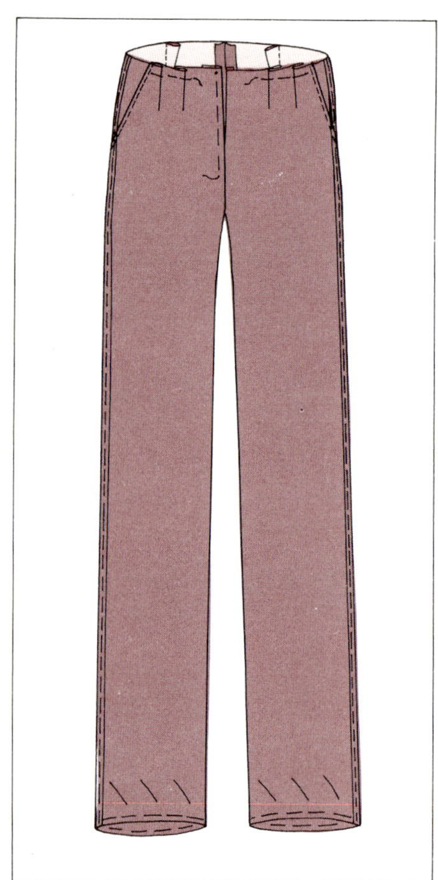

the waistband stiffening or a length of curved petersham, round your waist on top of the trousers and pin together.
If you did not machine the back darts earlier, check the fit now to see that their position, width and length are correct. Alter by pinning if necessary.
Next check the width of the leg again at thigh and hem level. It should be correct but alter it if necessary.
Look at the front pleats and the fit of the waist. If the trousers are too tight, snip the tacking and reduce the width of the pleats. If you have not made the inset pockets you can, if necessary, snip the side seam tacking and make the pleats smaller or possibly remove one completely. Pin out any surplus at side seam. This will give a flatter fit across the front. Look at the back waist, taking in the crutch seam at the centre back if the waist is too big.
Look at the fit of the crutch seam and pin out any surplus or snip tackings if it is tight anywhere. Mark the areas with chalk or pins so that you can re-tack on those marks for the next fitting.
Bagginess below the bottom indicates that the crutch must be scooped out. (First diagram, page 63.) At this stage note it and remember when re-tacking.
Tightness across the front at crutch level indicates that the front crutch curve needs releasing.
(Second diagram, page 63.)
If there is a lot of creasing at the

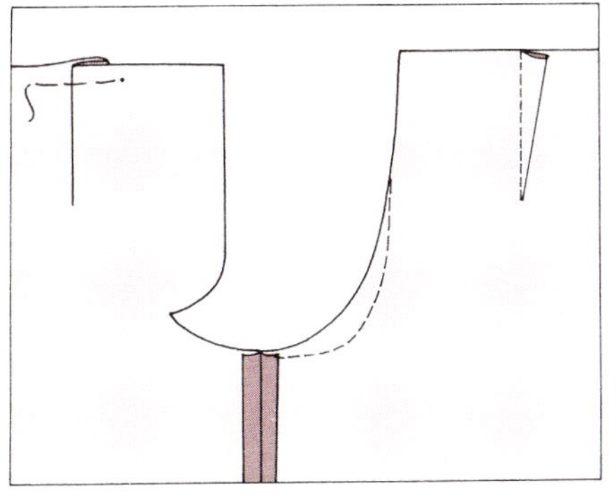

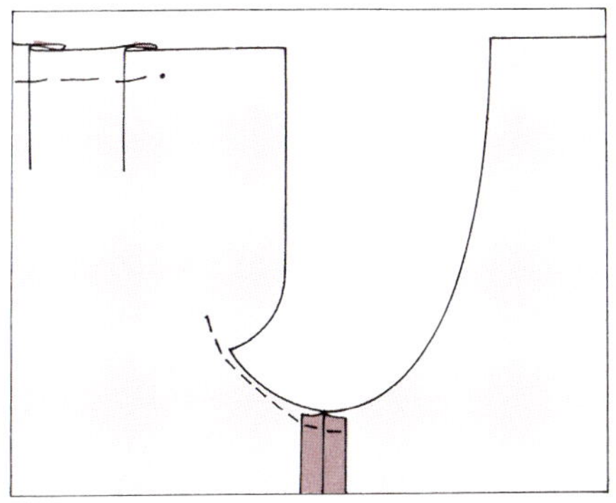

crutch it may be that the leg is tight at that level. If this is so, a triangle of fabric can be inserted into each inside leg seam. You can find out if this is needed by snipping the tacking of the inside leg seam to see if it pulls apart. Mark your waistline by chalking or pinning on the trousers at the lower edge of the petersham. Finally, look at the leg length and mark any adjustment necessary.
Remove petersham and the pins in the fly opening and take off the trousers. Make sure any alterations are clearly marked with chalk or tacking, including the waist level. Remove tacking from hems and undo the crutch seam to separate the legs. Remove the second row of tacking from the outside leg seams.
Turn the legs wrong side out. Machine inside leg and outside leg seams from top to hem. Press open and neaten the raw edges with zig-zag stitch.

Trouser creases
You may prefer no creases in soft fabrics but in most materials the trousers will hang better if creases are well pressed.
Hold one trouser leg up, right side out, by the hem; arrange leg seams with inside seam 1–2cm ($\frac{3}{8}$–$\frac{3}{4}$in) towards front. This places the front creases centrally over the knee and gives a better hang than when the seams are together. Arrange trousers right side up on pressing surface, with inside leg uppermost and front fold running from hem to waist running into the front pleat nearest to centre front. Use a damp cloth for all trouser pressing. Place the cloth over the front crease and press to a little way up the leg.
Remove iron and bang stream in with a block or if using a steam iron, run this over the area. Press across the leg from this point to establish back crease. Continue pressing the front and back crutch area. Complete front crease up to waist. Press back crease so that it meets centre back seam at waist. Press both legs. Hang them up to cool before continuing.

5 Crutch seam
At the waist, machine across the front pleats 1cm ($\frac{3}{8}$in) below the edge to hold them in. Place the legs together and tack the crutch seam as before but following any fitting marks made. Turn up the trouser hems, tack close to the fold and press. Baste round the leg to hold the hem surplus.
Fit Put on the trousers, pin up the zip opening, put the waist petersham or interfacing round, and pin and check the fit of the crutch seam. If the waist size needs adjusting alter the crutch seam at the waist. Also check the waist level marked previously to make sure it is correct. Re-mark if necessary. Check the leg length. Take off the trousers and machine crutch seam. Place a length of tape or seam tape between inside leg seam and zip point to prevent stretching in wear. Machine the seam with a straight stitch from the front to the inside leg, then change if you can to a slight zig-zag or stretch stitch to allow give in the seam. Alternatively, a triple stitch is suitable if you have it.
For strength, work an extra row of stitching close to the first, on the section where the tape comes. Remove tackings. Press the seam open from back waist down to the sharpest point of the crutch curve and from the zip point down to the inside leg seam. Do not snip the turnings, and do not attempt to press open the turnings right under the leg, as the trousers hang better if the legs are left together. Neaten the seam edges.

6 Zip-fly insertion
The extension on the pattern on the right trouser front allows the zip to be inserted by this method. The zip remains well covered even under the strain of sitting down. The wide edge also makes it easier to insert a heavy brass jeans zip if the fabric is suitable. Alternatively, the zip in the trousers can be inserted by one of the other methods as described for the skirts (see pages 31 and 40). Those methods produce a less obvious trouser fastening. If you have omitted the inset pockets and wish to insert the zip in the left side seam use a nylon, metal or concealed zip and follow instructions given for inserting in skirts.
Cut a piece of light iron-on interfacing and press it to the wrong side of the fly extension. Neaten the outer edge, stitching over interfacing and fabric. The inner edge should run on the centre front fold line.

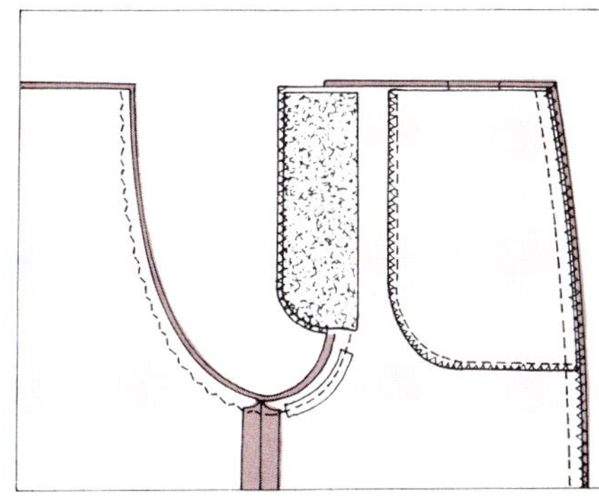

Note that this interfacing is not really necessary when making casual shorts. Turn under the fly extension and tack and press from waist edge to end of crutch seam.

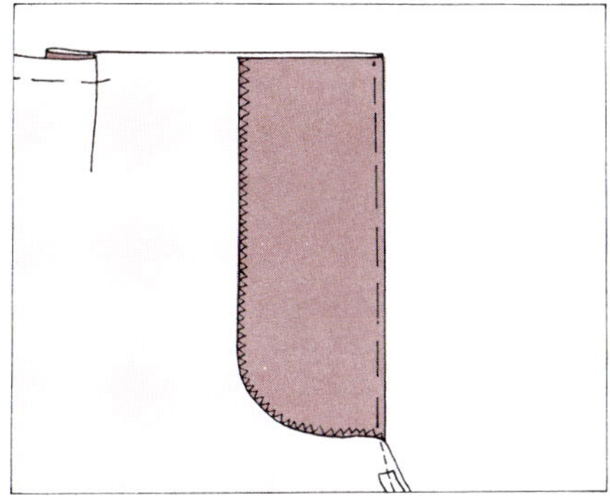

On the left trouser front, neaten the raw edge then turn under 1cm ($\frac{3}{8}$in). Tack and press. Extend this tacking 2.5cm (1in) below the base of the opening.
Note that on soft or floppy fabrics which are inclined to wrinkle, it helps to back this edge with light iron-on interfacing before you start.
Place the zip under this edge and hold it with the slider tab a little below the marked waistline. Place the folded edge close beside the teeth, tack and stitch. Either stitch by hand using prick stitch or attach the zip foot to the machine and stitch close to the fold. Stitch from the end of the tape at the base of this opening up to the waist.

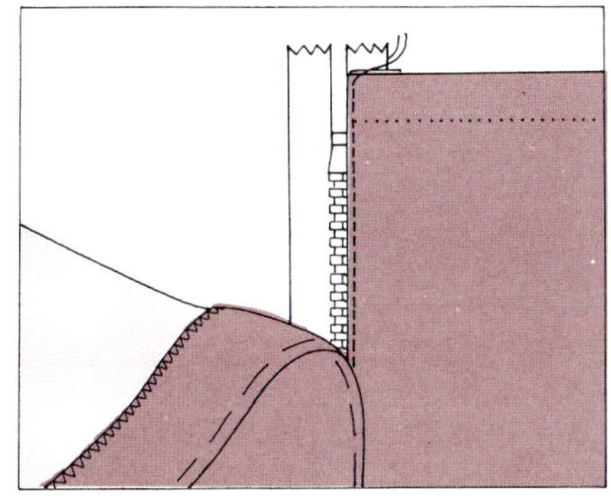

If the zip has a large slider and tab, stitch past it by raising the machine foot, leaving the needle in the fabric, and gently ease the slider down, undoing the zip. Lower the foot and complete the stitching.
Remove tackings. Press the stitching running the toe of the iron beside the teeth.
On the wrong side stitch again for strength, sewing the edge of the zip tape to the turning. This can be hand hemmed or machined. Do not stitch through to the outer layer of trousers.
Wrap the prepared wider edge over the zip and hold down so that the fold extends beyond the edge beneath by 5mm (¼in). Start at the base and catch the fold down to the trouser using tacking thread and an oversewing stitch. This will keep the fly in position while stitching. Tack again beside the zip teeth. Work with right side up but feel the position of the teeth with your fingers. Start from the base and work up to the waist.
Mark an accurate guide line on the right side with dots, using tailor's chalk or, better still, a chalk pencil. Do not use anything that will not easily brush off. Shape the stitching line at the base of the zip in a curve or at an angle making sure the guide line clears the bottom stop of the zip.
Stitch by machine or prick stitch by hand from the base to the waist. On the inside machine again for strength through the tape and the extension.
Remove all tacking, brush off the chalk, press the stitching with the toe of the iron.
On heavy fabrics work a small bar tack at the base of the opening.

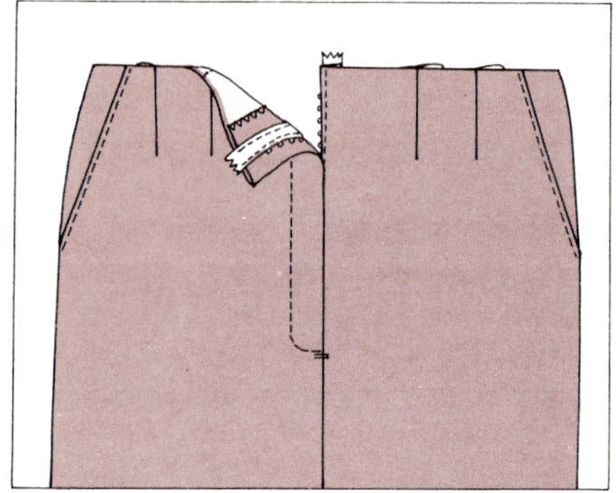

7 Waistband

Attach waistband interfacing to wrong side of waistband. Anchor by stitching down the centre in addition to the adhesive. Mark extension.
If you are using waistband stiffening that is only half the width of the fabric waistband, attach by machining along both edges or use herringbone stitch.
Hold trousers wrong side out and pin the overlap point on the band to match the zip opening on the left of the trousers. Pin the other end to match the front edge, leaving a seam allowance extending. Pin at intervals along the waistband. The seam allowance on the waistband is indicated by the edge of the stiffening. Insert the pins vertically.

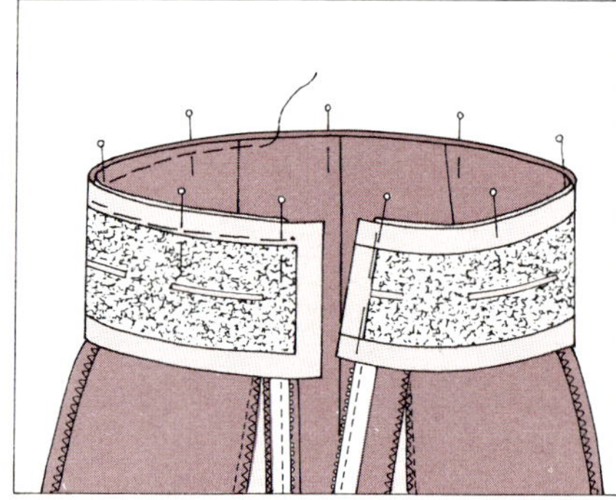

Tack the band to the garment, stitching just beside the edge of the stiffening. Remove pins. Machine on the tacking. Remove tacking.
Trim the seam allowance. Fold waistband up and press on both sides, pressing turnings up into the band.
Press band ends on to wrong side.

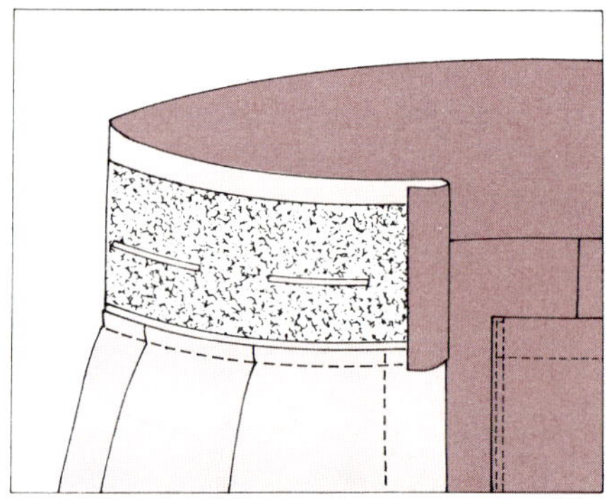

Fold the band in half and press. Bring the edge down on to the right side of the garment. Baste along band. Tuck under the raw edge so that it just covers the stitching.

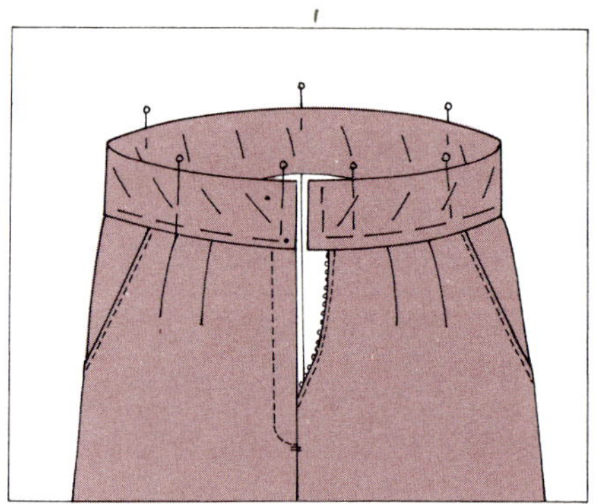

Pin vertically. Pin the underlap so that all edges meet. Tack all round pinned edges. Remove the pins. Press.
Work a row of machining all round the band with the right side uppermost. The stitching should be an even 2mm ($\frac{1}{16}$in) inside the edge. Use a straight or zig-zag stitch. Remove tackings. Press.

8 Hems

Remove all tacking from hems but leave a pin or chalk mark at the correct length.
Fold the trousers so that both legs lie flat together. Mark the hem length on the outside and inside leg seams.
With trouser leg right side out, turn in the surplus fabric and tack near the fold.
Remove pins and press the hem.

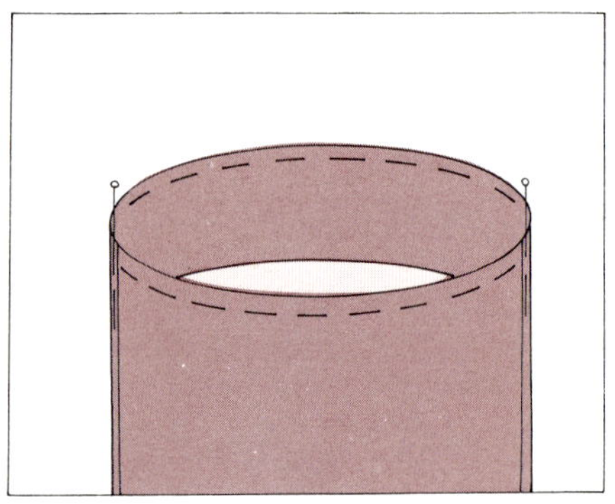

Arrange hem on pressing surface right side out and insert the toe of the iron, revolving the trouser leg as you press.

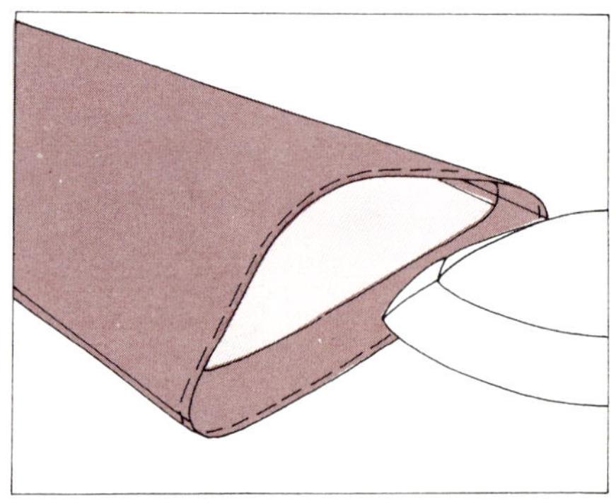

If you have an adjustable marker set it at 4cm (1½in). Mark the hem at this depth with chalk and trim off the surplus fabric. Neaten the raw edge.
For medium and heavy fabrics turn trouser leg wrong side out and slip adhesive web under the hem. The web is 3cm (1¼in) wide and will therefore be covered by the hem edge. Arrange the web carefully to ensure that it is flat and then put your hands inside the leg and pull outwards.

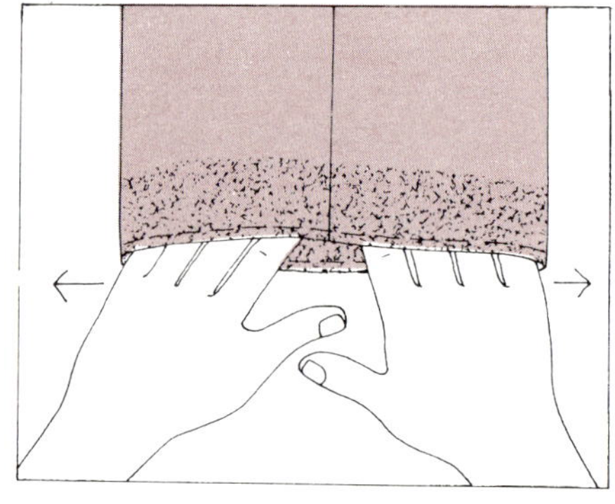

This ensures there is sufficient web in the hem and avoids the risk of it closing up and tightening the edge. Arrange the hem carefully over the sleeve board and press using a hot iron and a damp cloth. Press up to the neatened edge but not over it. Use the iron sideways and press with short sharp movements several times until the web has throughly melted.

Remove tackings, turn trousers right side out, re-fold the legs and re-press the creases in the lower part of the legs.

On light fabrics, work catch stitch loosely under the neatened edge but hem or herringbone for strength at the seams. Remove all tacking.

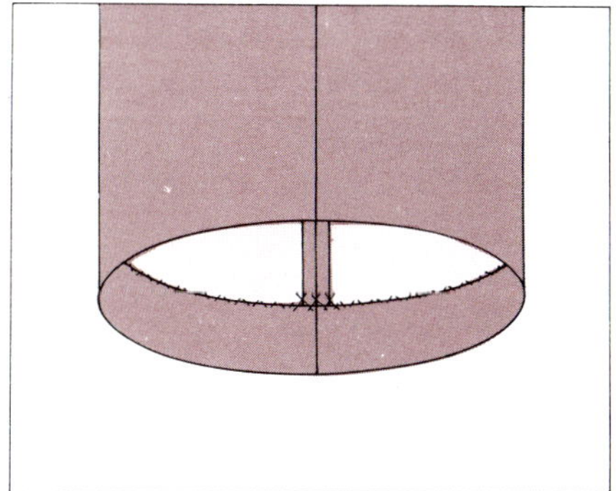

9 Waist fastening

Work a machine-made buttonhole horizontally in the end of the waistband, starting the width of the button in from the end of the band. Sew the button in position using double thread, waxed, and making a strong shank.

Alternatively attach another fastening such as a trouser clip or a length of Velcro.

KNEE-LENGTH SHORTS

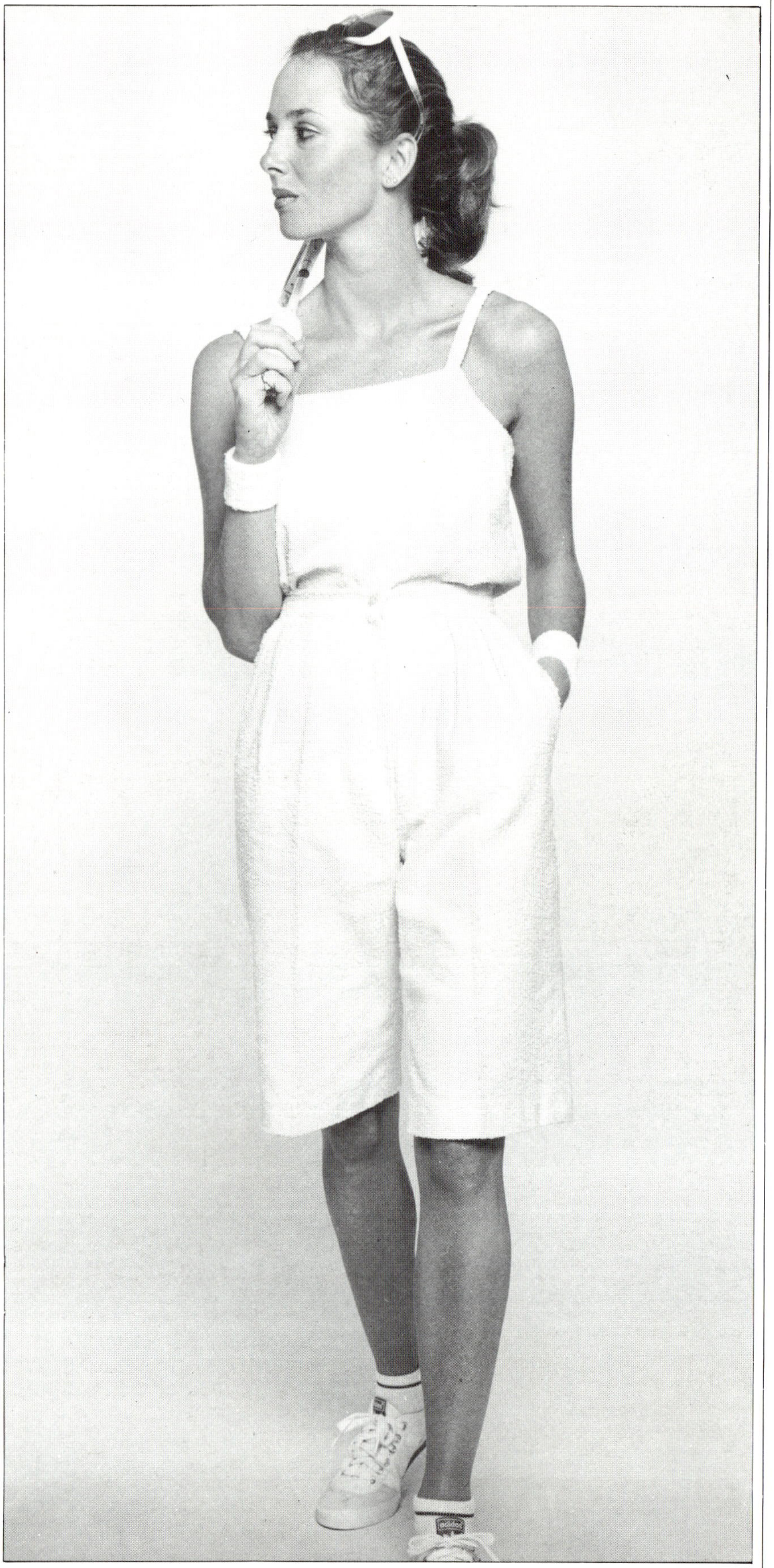

These are fashionable knee-length shorts made from the basic trouser pattern. We made them in pink towelling and teamed them with the camisole (page 68) also in towelling.

FABRICS

Use sporting or fashion fabrics including cotton drill, sailcloth, corduroy, flannel, tweed, velveteen, denim, towelling.

Quantities
These shorts will take less fabric than the trousers (page 60); each leg is just over 40cm (16in) shorter. Size 12 will take about 2.20m of 90cm (36in) fabric, or 2m of 115cm (45in) fabric.
Interfacing is needed to stiffen the waistband and for the patch pockets.
Attach light, iron-on interfacing to pocket facing piece.
If using heavy fabric reduce bulk by cutting the pocket facing in lining fabric.
Finished length, inside leg: 30.5cm (12in).

HABERDASHERY

- 2 reels thread
- 20cm (8in) metal or nylon zip or jeans zip
- Waistband interfacing
- Waistband fastening: 1 button
- Light iron-on interfacing for pocket
- Light interfacing strip for patch pockets

PATTERN PIECES

29, 30 cut on the knee-length line.
31, 32, 33 and 15.

MAKING UP

Make up the shorts following the instructions for the trousers (page 60) but omitting the instructions for reinforcing the crutch with seam tape. This is not necessary with shorts unless you are using stretch fabric.

SPORTS OR BEACH SHORTS

'Shorter' shorts for beach or sports have inset pockets and optional patch pockets on the back. All edges, including hems, are machine stitched.

FABRIC

Most lightweight fabrics are suitable, e.g. cotton, towelling or drill.

Quantities

Width	*Size*	*Quantity*
90cm (36in)	10	1.20m
	12	1.25m
	14	1.25m
	16	1.35m
	18	1.40m
115cm (45in)	10	0.95m
	12	0.95m
	14	1.10m
	16	1.10m
	18	1.10m

HABERDASHERY

2 reels thread

20cm (8in) nylon or metal zip or jeans zip

Waistband interfacing

Waistband fastening: 1 button

PATTERN PIECES

29 and 30 cut off or traced on shorts line.
31, 32, 33 and 15.

MAKING UP

Make up following instructions for trousers (page 60) but omit pocket interfacing. Also omit reinforcing the crutch seam with tape. This is not necessary with shorts.
Turn narrow hems on the legs and machine stitch to finish.

Fold fabric wrong sides together

90cm (36in) fabric	115cm (45in) fabric
Selvedges 31 29 30 33 32 15 Fold Open fabric out to cut piece 15	Selvedges 33 29 30 15 31 32 Fold Open fabric out to cut piece 15

CAMISOLE

This is a fashionable waist-length top with a shaped hem and bust darts. It has a short, slit opening at the back and the top edge is finished with a facing. It can be glamorous or practical and can be teamed with other garments in the book to make a complete outfit.

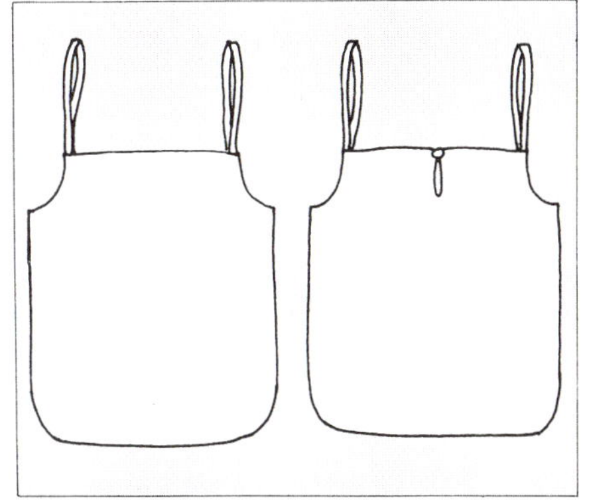

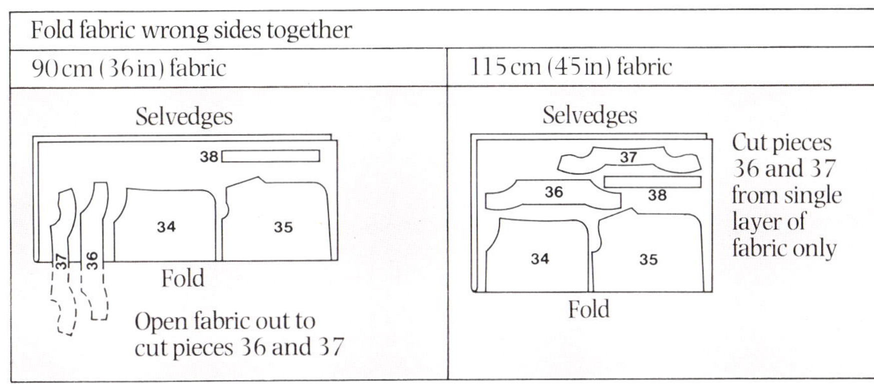

FABRIC

We made one camisole in towelling, one in jersey, and one in embossed silk but the simple style lends itself to a variety of lightweight fabrics: silk, satin, crêpe, cotton, lace, chiffon, brocade.

There are colour photographs showing the camisole in various fabrics on pages 38 and 55.

Quantities

Width	*Size*	*Quantity*
90cm (36in)	10	1.10m
	12	1.10m
	14	1.15m
	16	1.15m
	18	1.15m
115cm (45in)	10	0.90m
	12	0.90m
	14	0.90m
	16	0.90m
	18	0.95m

Transparent fabrics such as chiffon and voile should be mounted on to lining or on to another layer of the same fabric. Read the note at the end of this section for the technique.

Mounting requires the same amount of fabric again and this could be a conventional lining or something more comfortable such as cotton lawn.

Interfacing is needed for the top edge of the camisole and the straps. Use a light iron-on or sew-in variety.

HABERDASHERY

- 1 reel thread
- 1 small button
- Small piece adhesive web to hold facings in position
- Small piece paper-backed adhesive for slit facing

PATTERN PIECES

34, 35, 36, 37 and 38.

CUTTING OUT

Pin pieces 36, 37, 38 to interfacing and cut out.

Pin 34, 35, 36 and 37 to fabric following the layout diagram shown and cut out. Open out remaining fabric and press 38, strap interfacing, to wrong side making sure the grain is correctly placed.

If you prefer to have a straight hemline cut pieces 34 and 35 straight at the lower edge. The curved hemline may be difficult to turn up neatly on bulky fabric such as towelling.

If the camisole is to be mounted, cut out pieces 34 and 35 again in fabric or lining fabric.

Marking

Mark centre back and centre front folds with tacking on back, front and facings. Mark the stitching point of the curved hemline on the side seams.

MAKING UP

1 Straps

Begin by making the straps so that they can be used at the fitting.

Fold the interfaced straps right sides together and tack. Press lightly.

Locate the groove on your machine needle plate that is the width of the strap from the needle position. This is 1.5cm ($\frac{5}{8}$in) if you make them to the pattern width. Remember that the seam allowed on the strap is 5mm ($\frac{1}{4}$in). Place strap under machine foot with fold to the right, lined up with the groove and machine down the length and across one end.

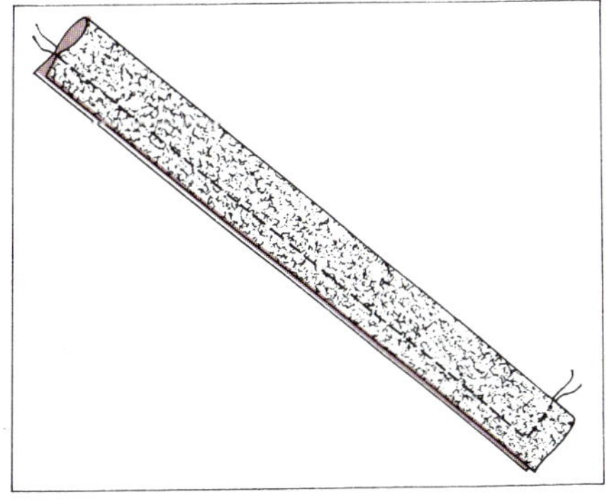

Trim the edges and cut away surplus at corners. Use the blunt end of a bodkin or the ball end of a rouleau turner to turn the straps right side out. Work out the join to the edge. Tack if fabric is springy. Press. If top stitching other edges of the camisole, top stitch the straps now.

The raw end of the strap is inserted between camisole and facing at the front. The other end is sewn inside the back after completing the facing.

Alternative straps

Wider straps may be made in order to cover bra straps more successfully. They will also wear better if you are using firm fabrics.

Cut lengths of light interfacing strip (which is 6cm (2$\frac{1}{2}$in) wide in total) equal to the length of the strap pattern. Press these to the wrong side of the fabric on the straight grain. Cut out round each strap, adding a small allowance on each long edge.

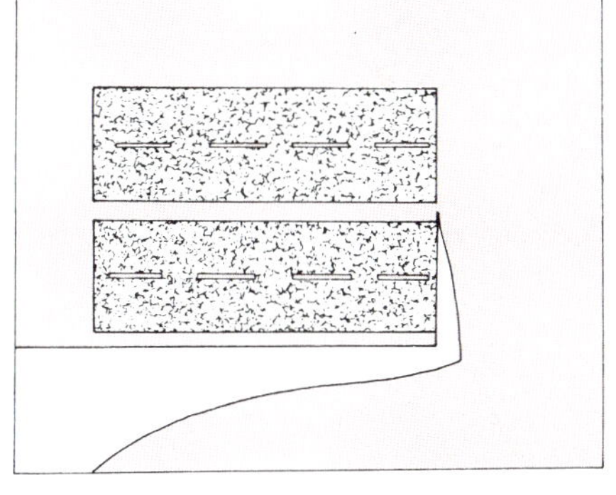

Fold straps right sides together and insert 4 pins with the heads extending beyond the fold. Place under machine foot and machine just off the edge of the interfacing and across one end.

Trim the turnings and cut away surplus fabric at corners. Use a bodkin or rouleau turner to turn straps right side out. Roll edge to work out the join and press.

Top stitch the straps and loop stitch across raw ends to neaten.

(Diagrams, page 70.)

2

Place interfacing to wrong sides of back and front sections and attach by basting or pressing to the upper edges.

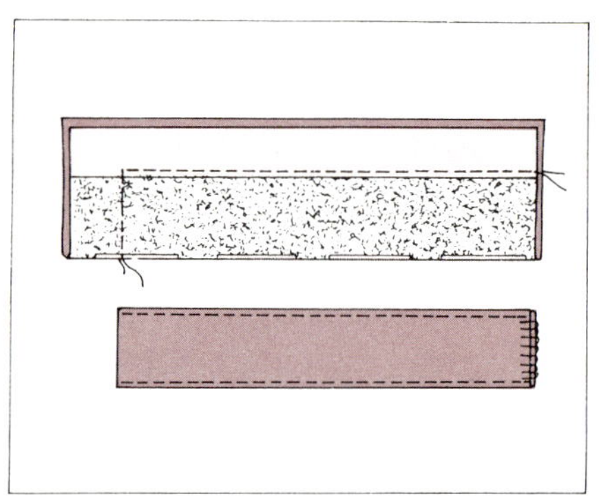

On the back press a narrow rectangle of paper-backed adhesive web to the centre and mark the length and position of the slit opening clearly with a row of dots made on the interfacing using chalk pencil.

3
Tack darts in front camisole; fold fabric wrong side out matching up the dart lines. Insert one pin across the dart near the raw edge and another below the point. Tack on the marks, finishing on the fold of the fabric. Remove pins.

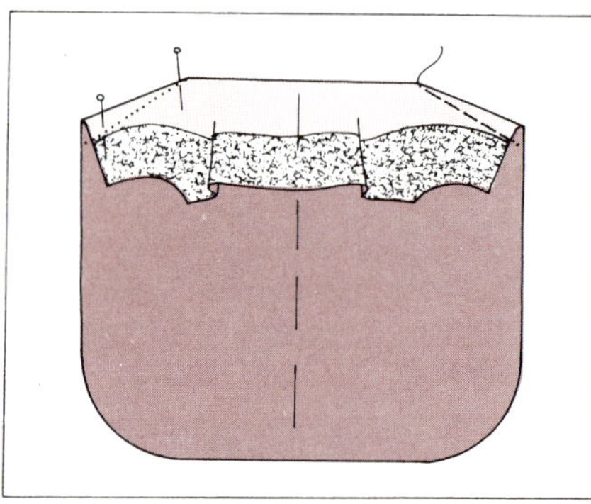

Place back and front camisole right sides together with side edges level. Taking 1.5cm ($\frac{5}{8}$in) seam allowances tack one side from underarm to hem point but leave the other one open at the underarm above the dart to allow for fitting.

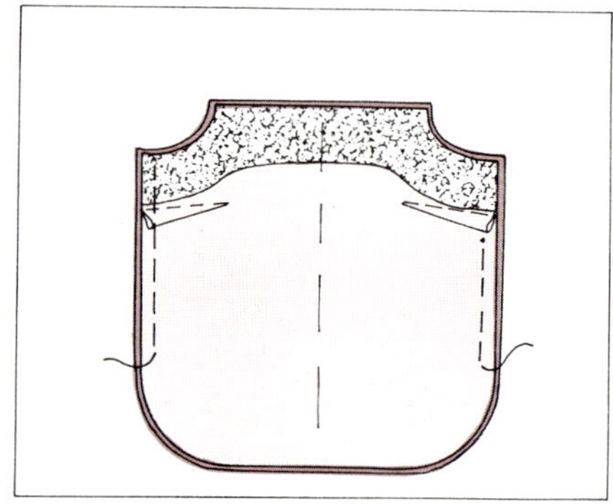

Turn camisole right side out, pin straps in position on the back on the right side, locating one side of the strap at the corner of the top edge.
Fit If you are planning to wear a particular bra with the camisole, put it on at this stage. Try on the camisole.

Bring the straps over to the front and pin at a comfortable level.
Check the length and level of the darts; they should be at bust level. If the darts need lowering, try adjusting the strap length. If this is insufficient then snip the tacking and re-pin the dart in a lower position. If the camisole feels restricting across the bust area, snip the tacking at the dart point to shorten it.
Check the fit of the camisole at underarm level and take it in or let it out at the side seams if necessary. If you have a narrow back you may have to pin out a little on the back at the seam edge, but not the front.
If the alterations are extensive it is easier to put the camisole on inside out so that you can pin the adjustments. Remember that there is still a seam allowance to come off the upper edge and underarm.
Take off the camisole. Re-tack any adjustments. Mark the exact length of strap required using tailor's chalk or pins. Remove all other pins, detach the straps and remove tacking from side seams.
Machine the darts from side edge to point and fasten off the stitching. Remove tackings. Press the darts with the bulk of the fabric lying down towards the hemline.

4 Side seams
Place camisole back and front right sides together. Tack from underarm to hemline point.
Stitch seams from marked position at hem to underarm or, if you have a straight hemline, stitch the entire seam.

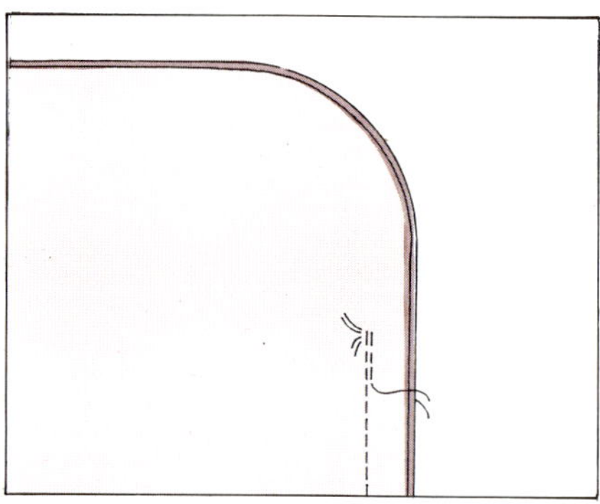

Remove tacks, press seam and neaten raw edges with zig-zag or overcasting. If your fabric is fine or fraying make French seams rather than open seams (see page 49).

5 Hem
Turn up and tack a narrow hem round the lower edge of front and back. With most fabrics you will be able to turn back 5mm ($\frac{1}{4}$in) and a further 1cm ($\frac{3}{8}$in). This will use the 1.5cm ($\frac{5}{8}$in) allowed on the pattern.

On fine fabrics make the hem as narrow as possible; the resulting extra length of camisole will not affect the finished effect.
Tack neatly round the curved edges, running the hem into the side seam turnings. Make a small snip which should be level with the base of the seam stitching to allow the hem to lie flat. Press the hem. Finish either by slip-hemming if fabric is fine or by machining. The machining can be worked in a continuous line by making a neat horizontal row of stitching across the side seam. Overcast the snipped raw edges of seam allowance.

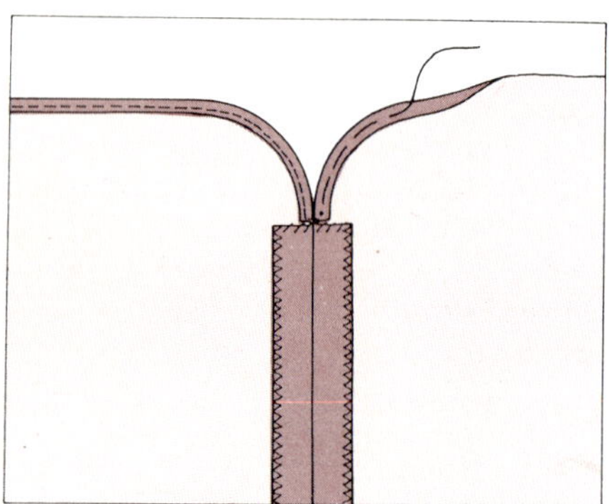

6 Back opening and facings
Place straps in position on right side of camisole at front with the raw ends level and the edge of the strap at the corner.
Machine across each strap 1cm ($\frac{3}{8}$in) in from edge to hold in position.
Place front facing to camisole right side down on top of straps. Match centre front marks and tack to within 2cm ($\frac{3}{4}$in) of the side seams.

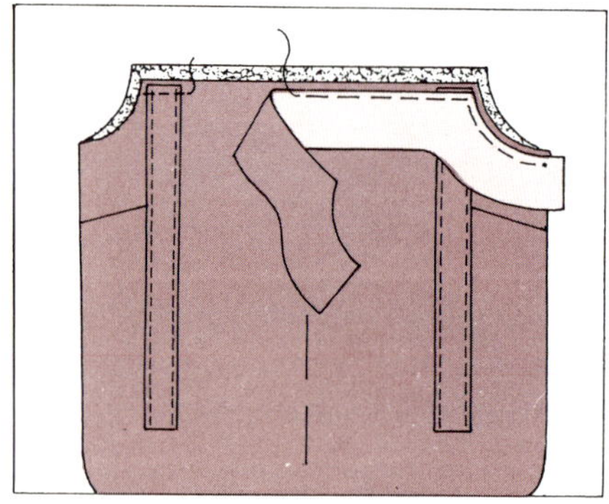

Place back facing in position right side down, matching centre back marks and tack. Press front and back facing edges at side seams so that folds meet. Stitch the facing join, trim and press open.
Machine all round top of camisole to attach facing, turning stitching down and beside the marked opening at centre back. The two rows of stitching should be about 5mm ($\frac{1}{4}$in) apart as for a faced slit opening. Stitch to form a point at the bottom.

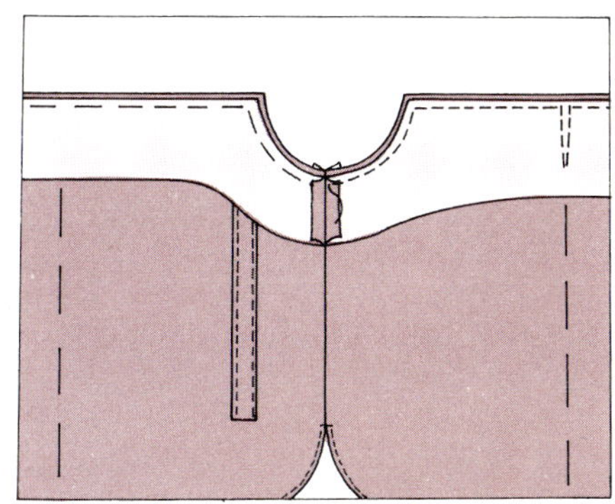

Trim and layer all raw edges. Snip the underarm curves, cut down the slit at the back. Roll facing to wrong side, roll the edges until the join is on the edge and the straps extend fully at the front. Tack the edge. Press. Trim the outer edge of the facing and neaten with zig-zag or overcasting. Where the facing crosses the side seam, hem or herringbone. Slip rectangles of adhesive web round the remainder of the facing between facing and fabric. Press. The adhesive applied when preparing the interfacing will melt and hold the facing down when pressed.

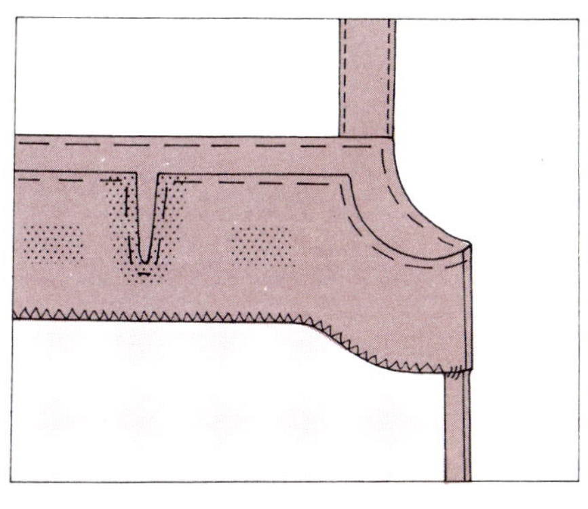

Leave edge tacking in place until completion. Add top stitching if you wish round upper edge, back opening and hemline.
Bring the ends of the straps into position at the back on the wrong side. Pin. Tack and try on to check the position. Hem along the edge of the camisole, down the sides of the strap and across the end. This allows for adjustment.

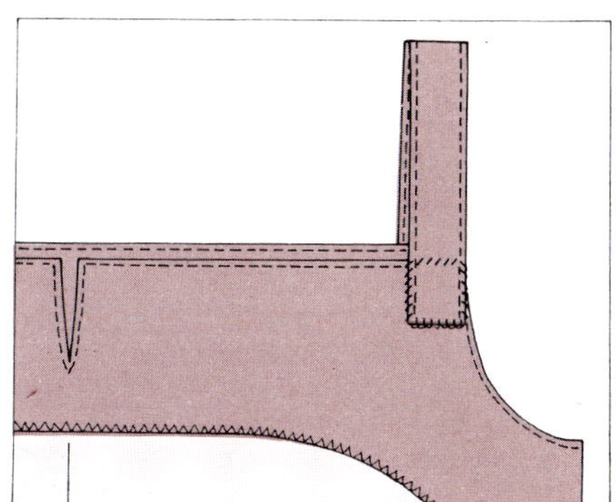

7 Fastening
The best fastenings are either a press stud, with one piece attached by only one hole and left to extend beyond the opening, or a button and thread loop.

Button and thread loop
Attach the button first, stitching it firmly to the left side of the opening 5 mm ($\frac{1}{4}$ in) in and 5 mm ($\frac{1}{4}$ in) down from the corner. Thread needle with a fairly long piece of thread, double knot it and run beeswax along it once. Insert needle on wrong side, between facing and garment. Bring the needle up near the garment edge. Take another stitch to bring the needle out at the corner.
Wind thread round button and insert needle in fold below. Check the thread loop is correct size to hold edges together and slip over button; remove thread from button. Work three more loops the same size.
Work loop stitch closely along the thread to cover and make it firm. Fasten off on the inside. Cut off the knot. Press the camisole to finish.

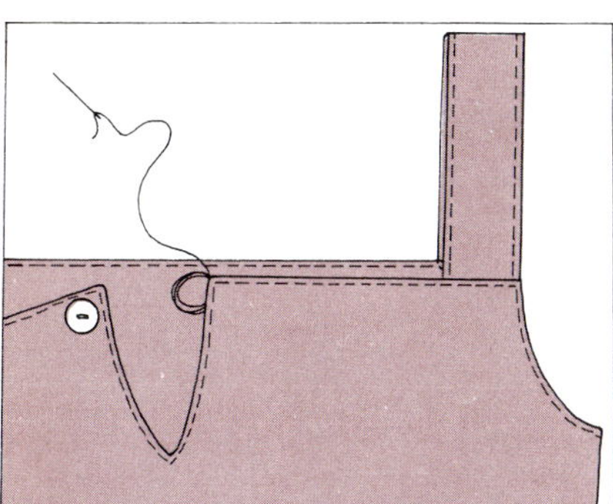

On some figures, especially the larger busted, it may be advisable to add a short piece of narrow-width elastic at the underarm section.
Cut the elastic 2.5 cm (1 in) shorter than the underarm curved section. Place it on the inside of the camisole at the edge. Use a zig-zag or stretch stitch to machine over it, stretching the elastic to fit.

Straight hemline
A straight hem can be finished with a narrow machined or hemmed edge or, on some light fabrics, try turning under a narrow single turning and working a close zig-zag stitch or shell edge stitch. If using jersey the edge can be stretched to make it flute attractively. Finish by trimming off surplus edge of fabric on the wrong side.

Mounting
To make the camisole of double fabric or one layer of fabric on lining, mark darts, etc., on the under layer only. Place each under-layer on the table marked side downwards. Place outer fabric on top wrong side down and, starting at the centre, work rows of basting stitches all over each piece. Mount back and front. Facings should be made from top fabric only. Strap may be mounted before interfacing is added. Make up the camisole as instructed, treating it as one layer of fabric. Remove basting when camisole is finished and press.

Photographs: ROBYN BEECHE
Diagrams: JIL SHIPLEY

The author and the BBC would like to thank several people for their help with this book: Hilda Cawood, Myra Davidson, Sue Lemon, Dorothy Longden, Mary Peacock and Cita Wood.

They would also like to thank the following manufacturers and shops for lending accessories for the photographs:
Hats Frederick Fox, Edward Mann
Berets Kangol
Belts and bags Fenwicks, Mulberry Co., Christopher Trill
Shoes Charles Jourdan, Russell and Bromley, Olympic Way at Harrods
Jewellery Liberty's, Fenwicks, Adrien Mann
Scarves and gloves Liberty's
Sports accessories Olympic Way at Harrods
Towels Harrods
Tights Mary Quant
Sunglasses and ties Mulberry Co.

Photographic stylist:
Christine Woolnough